THE UNIVERSITY OF WINCHESTER

Martial Rose Library
Tel: 01962 827306

OXFORD SHAKESPEARE TOPICS
Published and Forthcoming Titles Include:

Oxford Shakespeare Topics

GENERAL EDITORS: PETER HOLLAND AND STANLEY WELLS

Shakespeare and the Drama of his Time

MARTIN WIGGINS

OXFORD

UNIVERSITY PRESS

OXFORD
UNIVERSITY PRESS

Great Clarendon Street, Oxford OX2 6DP
Oxford University Press is a department of the University of Oxford.
It furthers the University's objective of excellence in research, scholarship,
and education by publishing worldwide in

Oxford New York

Athens Auckland Bangkok Bogotá Buenos Aires Calcutta
Cape Town Chennai Dar es Salaam Delhi Florence Hong Kong Istanbul
Karachi Kuala Lumpur Madrid Melbourne Mexico City Mumbai
Nairobi Paris São Paulo Shanghai Singapore Taipei Tokyo Toronto Warsaw
and associated companies in Berlin Ibadan

Oxford is a registered trade mark of Oxford University Press
in the UK and certain other countries

Published in the United States
by Oxford University Press Inc., New York

British Library Cataloguing in Publication Data
Data available

Library of Congress Cataloging in Publication Data
Wiggins, Martin.
 Shakespeare and the drama of his time / Martin Wiggins.
  p. cm. — (Oxford Shakespeare topics)
 Includes bibliographical references (p.) and index.

  1. English drama—Early modern and Elizabethan, 1500–1600—History and criticism. 2.
 Shakespeare, William, 1564–1616—Contemporaries. 1. Title. 11. Series
 PR651.W49 2000 822'.309—dc21 00–024418
 ISBN 0–19–871161–1
 ISBN 0–19–871160–3 (pbk.)

10 9 8 7 6 5 4 3 2 1

Typeset by Kolam Information Services Pvt Ltd, Pondicherry, India
Printed in Great Britain
on acid-free paper by
Biddles Ltd. Guildford and Kings Lynn

Acknowledgements

This book could not have been written without Stanley Wells, and not only because he invited me to do so in the first place: I am grateful to him for his patience and his judicious suggestions for fine-tuning. Robert Smallwood and Frances Whistler kindly helped me through the worst delirium of writer's block and read sections of the book in draft, and I have profited from every one of their suggestions. My students at the Shakespeare Institute have been more supportive than I had any right to expect, and the members of the Renaissance Drama Research Group have been a constant source of intellectual stimulation and companionship. For their contributions great and small I also owe thanks to Roberta Barker, Stephanie Gamble, Chiaki Hanabusa, Peter Holland, Peter Hinds, John Jowett, Margaret Jane Kidnie, Jane Kingsley-Smith, Christian van Nieuwerburgh, Renata Oggero, Rebekah Owens, James Purkis, and Katie Ryde; and, since a book like this is bound to have been longer in the conception even than it was in the writing, I must make special acknowledgement of my long-standing debt to the outstanding teachers with whom I first studied English Renaissance drama, John Creaser, John Wilders, and Emrys Jones. All errors, misjudgements, and other blemishes are mine alone.

The book is dedicated to Kelley Costigan, for making it possible.

Contents

The Permeable Bard

In his own time, William Shakespeare was one author among many. There are just under 250 extant plays written for the commercial theatre during the period roughly corresponding with his career, of which he wrote thirty-eight; many more have not survived, including another two of his, *Love's Labours Won* and *Cardenio.* John Webster gives a handy survey of the profession in the preface to his tragedy, *The White Devil* (1612), which lists all but one of the important writers then working in the theatre:

that full and heightened style of Master Chapman; the laboured and under-standing works of Master Jonson; the no less worthy composures [com-positions] of the both worthily excellent Master Beaumont and Master Fletcher; and lastly (without wrong last to be named) the right happy and copious industry of Master Shakespeare, Master Dekker, and Master Heywood.

(The missing person, incidentally, is Thomas Middleton.) Along with John Marston, who had left the theatre a few years earlier, this was the 'Jacobean generation' of dramatists; there was also an 'Elizabethan generation', including Greene, Peele, Marlowe, Kyd, and Lyly, who were all established when Shakespeare started (and all dead when Webster wrote).

This was a relatively small group of people, all working in the same industry and in the same city. Naturally they knew one another and worked both in competition and together; Marlowe and Kyd even shared accommodation at one point. Often two or more of them would collaborate: typically a play would be divided up in the planning stages, and each contributor would take responsibility for writing a designated group of not necessarily contiguous scenes. Around 15 per cent of the 250-odd surviving plays of the 'Shakespearian' period were written like this. More broadly, dramatists would also have seen and learned from one another's plays, not least because they needed to know what would best attract paying audiences.

Watching Shakespeare's impact on some of his lesser contemporaries can offer a certain sardonic amusement to readers so inclined. For example, in the domestic murder play, *A Warning for Fair Women* (*c*.1598), a character drops into the register of romantic love—'Yonder she sits to light this obscure street | Like a bright diamond worn in some dark place' (343–4)—and there is something unintentionally comic about the anonymous author's striving to achieve the effect, and yet avoid the precise words, of *Romeo and Juliet* (1595–6): 'It seems she hangs upon the cheek of night | As a rich jewel in an Ethiope's ear.' (1. 5. 44–5) Those who laugh loudest, though, will probably be disconcerted by another example of this kind of verbal seepage between texts. It starts in the anonymous historical tragedy, *The Troublesome Reign of King John* (*c*.1588), when the dying King is carried onto the stage and commands his bearers, 'Set down, set down the load not worth your pain' (13. 1), and this time Shakespeare was the borrower. He reworked the line in *Richard III* (1592–3) when Lady Anne halts King Henry VI's funeral procession ('Set down, set down your honourable load', 1. 2. 1), before borrowing it again from himself in *As You Like It* (1600), when Orlando brings on the old but still living Adam to Duke Senior's forest table ('Welcome. Set down your venerable burden', 2. 7. 167); evidently it had stuck in his mind. (So, indeed, had the play: he adapted it as his own *King John* in the mid-1590s.) There is many another example of the phenomenon in his work; yet this easily demonstrable fact, that Shakespeare imitated other dramatists just as they imitated him, often meets with resistance.

One reason is that Shakespeare, once part of a group, has been reduced over time to pre-eminent singularity— and it is easy, though obviously mistaken, to assume that his plays are bound always to be the originals because they are the more familiar. As the seventeenth century wore on, most of the other dramatists of his time began to drop away into oblivion. Sir John Suckling's comedy, *The Goblins* (1638), includes a sequence in which a would-be poet is kidnapped by bandits, who persuade him that he has died and been transported to

Hades. He decides to check out the local worthies, and 'asks much after certain British blades, one Shakespeare, and Fletcher' (3.7. 136–7); the bandits cannot provide such eminence, but they do later offer 'he that writ *Tamburlaine*' (4. 5. 12). Primarily this is a joke about the gap between courtly and plebeian standards of literary taste, but it also illustrates the gradual demise of Shakespeare's professional context in later cultural history: the bandits (and probably Suckling too) don't *know* who wrote *Tamburlaine*; and before long, few people would even know of *Tamburlaine* itself, let alone its author, Marlowe. By the Restoration, Shakespeare was part of a trinity alongside Jonson and Fletcher, and they too were soon outstripped. Since the eighteenth century, Shakespeare has been more widely accessible, in print and on the stage, than any of his contemporaries.

It is easy to suppose that the other playwrights were whittled away by some literary equivalent of natural selection, that Shakespeare became a perennial best-seller through a timeless superiority of vision which keeps his work constantly meaningful for later generations. In fact, recent research has shown that it was a more contingent process, the details of which are far beyond the scope of this book. (Interested readers should consult Michael Dobson's 1992 monograph, *The Making of the National Poet*, for a seminal account.) What is important here is that Shakespeare became known as England's single greatest dramatist for reasons that had more to do with the cultural and political climate of later times than with a serious assessment of relative literary merit; and that the outcome was to naturalize his plays and push his contemporaries even further into unconsidered obscurity. Elizabethan and Jacobean drama was divided into a pair of neat categories, 'Shakespearian' and 'non-Shakespearian', each with a different status and a different set of attributed characteristics. Shakespeare finally came to cultural centrality towards the end of the eighteenth century, and was construed in terms of Romantic critical theory as a genius of unbounded personal creativity whose works arose from his own observation and imagination, unadulterated by formal literary influence; he also acquired the epithet 'the Bard', after the native Welsh poets who were thought to share the same traits. 'Non-Shakespearian' drama, meanwhile, was rescued from being a minority, antiquarian interest with the birth of historicist criticism, when scholars realized its usefulness in elucidating Shakespeare's obscurities: it emerged as a subsidiary topic whose wider importance was defined by its cultural and chronological proximity to the separable, primary topic of Shakespeare.

These notions, formulated two centuries ago, still inform the latent conceptual structures within which many people think about English Renaissance drama: that is what makes them uncomfortable with the possibility that Shakespeare was in any way indebted to his 'non-Shakespearian' contemporaries. We assume a 'Bard' who was impermeable to such influences because tradition has created a myth of his absolute originality and effortless superiority, and because the assumption of his primacy is embedded deep in the foundations of modern literary culture. Yet it is an assumption which ignores everything we know about the occupational circumstances of play-writing in his time. It depends on the notion that Shakespeare either worked in isolation from other dramatists, writing in some lonely garret like an archetypal Romantic poet, or that he had a superhuman (and probably professionally intolerable) ability to resist other people's thoughts and ideas. It seems far more likely that, as a theatre professional, he worked closely with his colleagues. In fact, five of the period's collaborative plays belong to the conventional Shakespeare canon (namely *Henry VI, Part 1*, *Timon of Athens*, *Pericles*, *Henry VIII*, and *The Two Noble Kinsmen*); it is also increasingly accepted that Shakespeare contributed scenes to the anonymous *Edward III* (*c.*1592), and perhaps to others too.

Of course, it is quite possible to construct an artistic personality for Shakespeare, founded on the fact that in his historical person he was a separate individual (born in Stratford and not Canterbury, like Marlowe; born in 1564 and not 1572, like Jonson), and drawing on the evidence of the plays he did and did not write. It is undeniable that he had certain distinctive authorial specialisms—notably English history plays—and that, conversely, there were kinds of drama which he avoided writing: he did not write adventure plays about popular English folk heroes, like *Guy, Earl of Warwick* (anonymous, 1592–3) or *George-a-Greene* (Robert Greene, 1590), or satirical comedies about contemporary London life, like *Eastward Ho* (Jonson, Chapman, and Marston, 1605) or *The Roaring Girl* (Middleton and Dekker, 1611), or sardonic tragedies about corrupt foreign courts, like *The Revenger's Tragedy* (Middleton, 1606) or *The Duchess of Malfi* (Webster, 1614). Yet in most respects there are more generic similarities than differences between his work and that of his contemporaries. Every so often nowadays there is a flurry of media activity over some ill-advised but well-orchestrated attempt to attribute to him some anonymous play of the time, and reporters will often put it to experts that it *sounds* a lot like Shakespeare. To the untrained ear, a very great deal of Elizabethan and Jacobean drama sounds like Shakespeare. Though it can be meaningful to differentiate between him and his great contemporaries, it is even more meaningful to consider them together—and to do so, recognizing the extent to which they enabled one another's work, does not in any way make Shakespeare a lesser artist.

So when I was asked to write a book for this series entitled *Shakespeare and the Drama of his Time*, the thing that gave me misgivings was the word *and*: it posits a binary where it would be more accurate to see a continuum. In other words, it is a title which promises a study of the relationship between two bodies of material, the 'Shakespearian' and the 'non-Shakespearian', which were not distinct until later cultural history made them so. Shakespeare's plays would then become the book's conceptual bottle-neck: its argument would have to focus on specific points of permeation where they were significantly influenced by the 'non-Shakespearian' activity around them. That is obviously a part of my subject, but I have taken a broader view. The first three chapters deal with a series of fundamental historical changes in drama, each with an epicentre roughly ten years after the last: the emergence of the London theatre industry in the late 1570s and of new kinds of first tragedy, then comedy in the late 1580s and 1590s respectively. Chapter 5 deals with a similar, but more diffuse phenomenon, the development of tragicomedy in the early seventeenth century. In between, the fourth chapter is the book's interlude, the point where the non-linear dimension of aesthetics intersects with its otherwise predominantly historical trajectory: it is a wheel within the wheel, concerned not with drama's larger transformations and developments but with the details of the creative and artistic process that was the art of play-writing in the period. Throughout the book, Shakespeare's plays, as an important part of the drama of his time, are always present but never systematically placed as the sole objects of influence. A brief afterword considers their corresponding influence on his contemporaries and successors.

There is a lot of Elizabethan and Jacobean drama out there, even though not much of it is available these days. I have deliberately cast my net widely, which has meant going well beyond the selection of plays which can be seen in the theatre or read in accessible modernized editions. (All quotations have, however, been modernized.) A list of the editions to which act-, scene-, and line-numbers are keyed appears at the end of the book. The dates given for plays are those of their composition or, where known, first performance rather than their publication. I hope that in adopting this breadth of reference I have managed to communicate something of the range, the richness, and the complexity, of the 'non-Shakespearian' drama which is Shakespeare's inextricable historical context.

1

'The Causes of Plays'

Where did Elizabethan drama come from? It seems to spring fully-formed into existence in the 1580s, with the delicate, witty comedies of Lyly serving as a happy prologue to the triumphant entry of Kyd, Marlowe, and Shakespeare. Before them, English drama appears to have consisted mainly of quasi-allegorical plays preaching the dour Tudor lessons of continence, obedience, and strict, disciplinary child-rearing. When *The Spanish Tragedy*, *Doctor Faustus*, and *Richard III* were new, the theatre had no repertory of established classics, whereas those plays and others like them were perennials of the Jacobean and Caroline stage long after their original audiences had disappeared into history. The contrast between the generations seems absolute, with the younger Elizabethans enjoying a sudden plenitude of dramatic riches undreamed of by their mid-century forefathers.

The earliest attempt to answer this question of origins was made in 1582, when the Oxford-educated former playwright, Stephen Gosson, published a book which offered readers 'a taste ... of the causes of plays'. They arose, he suggested, as an indirect result of the English Reformation, and in particular the Elizabethan Settlement of 1559. The conversion of England from a Catholic to a Protestant nation gave a boost to its spiritual health which, according to Gosson, caused consternation elsewhere: 'the devil, foreseeing the ruin of his kingdom, both invented these shows and inspired men with devices [subject matter] to set them out, the better thereby to enlarge his dominion and pull us from God'.

Today this metaphysical conspiracy theory of literary history just looks batty, though in his own time Gosson was considered sane enough to proceed to a moderately successful ecclesiastical career. The intellectual content of his book does not differ significantly from the many other condemnations of the theatre which thundered from London's pulpits, presses, and chambers of municipal government. Drama was a fit instrument for its diabolic purpose, he argued, not only because its end was 'sinful delight', but also because of the deleterious social and psychological effects of its content: tragedies were full of 'wrath, cruelty, incest, injury, murder', while comedies presented 'love, cozenage [deceitful tricks], flattery, bawdry, sly conveyance of whoredom'; even if audiences did not leave the playhouse determined to imitate these bad examples, they were liable to grow melancholy ('lovers of dumps and lamentation') or turn into idle hedonists ('lovers of laughter and pleasure without any mean'). But what makes Gosson distinctive is his having spent about two years as a professional scriptwriter in the industry he now denounced.

This background gave him not only an insider's information but also a more literary prose style than his fellow antitheatricalists, and a clearer sense of narrative. His explanation of drama is itself like a play: it has an escalating sequence of events driven by a leading character, Satan. (Gosson himself also features in the minor role of reformed prodigal, a stereotype bound to appeal to pious Londoners of the time.) The assault on England falls into two distinct phases, beginning with the import of vice from the heart of Catholic Europe: 'First he sent over many wanton Italian books, which, being translated into English, have poisoned the manners of our country with foreign delights.' Drama then enters the scene in order to widen the devil's net: aware that not everyone could read this 'Italian bawdry', he devised 'comedies cut by the same pattern, which drag such a monstrous tail after them as is able to sweep whole cities into his lap'. Gosson's interpretation of history is so bizarre, his rhetoric in support of that interpretation so passionately powerful, that it is easy to overlook the accuracy of his perception of the history itself: his information is broadly correct—early Elizabethan prose fiction was indeed dominated by translations from Italian—and the overall structure of his narrative reflects the common practice of Elizabethan dramatists, transforming literary sources into plays. The supposed diabolic provenance of those sources and those plays should be incidental, to us if not to Stephen Gosson himself.[1]

Gosson's importance to us is two-fold: it lies in the facts that he writes about and in the fact that he should have written at all. His book, *Plays Confuted in Five Actions*, shows that the emergence of drama was a phenomenon which was felt to require explanation even before there had been performed a single one of the plays we now consider the classics of the Elizabethan stage; and this must complicate our notion of the suddenness with which those classics appeared. The 1570s is a dark period in the history of English drama not because few plays were written but because few have survived: from the entire decade there remain texts of only seven plays which might have been written for public performance. Gosson's own output is a case in point. He seems to have been a popular playwright: it cannot only have been personal and controversial reasons that prompted the revival of two of his older plays, *The Comedy of Captain Mario* and *Praise at Parting*, in the early 1580s. But this is not a matter we can judge for ourselves, for none of his dramatic work survives: theatre companies were understandably reluctant to release successful plays for publication, and Gosson himself would scarcely have done so either.

Those seven surviving plays are not only few but unrepresentative. Gosson's comments on tragedy and comedy bear witness to the generic diversity the theatre had achieved by the time he left it in 1579: these were plays which evidently bore some similarity to the kind of drama Marlowe and Shakespeare were writing a decade or so later. Yet the texts that got into print were mostly old-fashioned allegorical moralities with earnest titles like *The Conflict of Conscience* and *All for Money*, some of them equipped with handy if occasionally over-optimistic doubling plans showing how the plays could be performed by (usually) six actors. Presumably they were published not only for the instruction of readers but also for the convenience of players—in particular, probably, small, provincial touring troupes. In the capital, audience tastes were apparently rather more sophisticated.

So Elizabethan drama only seems to loom out of nowhere because in its mature state it has been better preserved than the plays which might have illustrated its earlier development. All that remains for us to go on is a clutch of information about titles and subject matter, along with occasional illuminating comments by Gosson and others. There is simply not enough evidence to support an 'evolutionary' analysis relating the plays of Shakespeare's time to their immediate antecedents; but that is not to say that we shall have to reconcile ourselves to absolute ignorance.

However much playwrights may be influenced by the practice of their contemporaries and predecessors, drama is never an entirely self-begotten phenomenon. From Gosson's time to Shakespeare's and beyond, it was moulded by a complex of material and cultural circumstances: plays were 'caused' by the institutions which supported their writing and production, by the ideas and traditions which contributed to their creation, and by the needs and desires they came into being to fulfil. So even when we cannot read or watch the finished product, we can still inspect some aspects of the mould: we may not always know precisely what the plays were like, but we can consider why they were written, what they were made of, and what they were for.

Theatre in Renaissance England

Gosson's opportunities to write, both for and against the stage, arose from the same set of circumstances. The years 1575–7 saw commercial theatre in London transformed by the appearance of several permanent, purpose-built playhouses in the suburbs and ecclesiastical liberties of the city. An earlier attempt at such a venture, the Red Lion in Stepney, seems not to have lasted long after its doors opened in 1567, but its successor, the Theatre, built in Shoreditch in 1576, remained operational for more than twenty years; the earliest public performances of, among others, *Romeo and Juliet*, *The Merchant of Venice*, and *Henry IV*, were given under the afternoon sun in this open-air amphitheatre modelled on the animal-baiting rings of Southwark. Its near neighbour, the Curtain, opened in 1577 and was probably the playhouse being used by Shakespeare's company in the winter of 1598–9 when they first presented *Henry V*.

Given that one prominent branch of moralistic opinion regarded playhouses as nothing less than chapels of Satan, it is not surprising that the arrival of so many in so brief a time should have made the late 1570s and early 1580s a bullish period for antitheatrical controversy: Gosson was only the best informed and most literary contributor to a little industry of sermons, ballads, and pamphlets. But the coming of the theatres also had more immediate consequences which are apparent in the historian and topographer William Harrison's gloomy remark, 'It is an evident token of a wicked time when players wax so rich that they can build such houses.'[2] The Theatre and the Curtain were an epoch in the commercial history of the English stage: they were a major investment of capital which helped to give drama, hitherto a peripatetic activity performed on *ad hoc* stages at fairs and inns, a more stable economic and institutional infrastructure. Players, or at least those at the top of their profession, were no longer shiftless, travelling vagabonds but established businessmen with their own premises, almost like shopkeepers.

If the playhouses gave the wealthier companies a local habitation, it was up to authority to give them a name. Early Elizabethan actors were vulnerable not only to the censure of the godly but also to a widespread cultural fear of 'masterless men' who had no place in society's hierarchical mechanisms of control. Such prejudices lay behind the period's strict vagrancy laws, first enacted in 1572, under which rogues, vagabonds, and sturdy beggars were liable, for success- ive offences, to be flogged, branded, and finally hanged. 'Common players' were expressly included in the Act's scope, unless they were retainers of a peer of the realm.[3] Of course, some companies already were: since the previous century, theatrically-inclined aristocrats had maintained troupes of players to provide entertainment for special occasions, both in their own households and as their contribution to the royal court's revels. During periods when they were not required for such duties, the actors would tour, and the name of a noble patron was often useful to impress a potentially hostile local magistrate. After 1572, it was essential: by making patronage a legal requirement, the Act brought the potentially eccentric, 'masterless' anomaly of the profes- sional theatre firmly into the recognized structure of society, and in so doing made an important contribution to its developing institutional stability.

To say that, more than anything else, the new playhouses needed plays is not entirely to state the obvious. Touring companies could survive with a limited stock of scripts, taking the same plays around the country to new audiences. The London-based companies, per- forming for a constant, albeit large, pool of potential theatregoers, had to vary their repertory. Continuous runs of a single play were uncom- mon; none is known before 1624, when Thomas Middleton's political satire, *A Game at Chess*, played for nine consecutive days before the authorities closed it down. Normally the companies would present a different play each day, announcing it from the stage after the previous afternoon's performance and on playbills stuck on street-corner posts, the advertising billboards of the time. The records of the theatre financier Philip Henslowe, dating from the 1590s, show the extent of the literary turnover: in the course of a year an established company would perform thirty or more plays in rotation, though not all of them would be new. We don't know how precisely that reflects the situation twenty years earlier, when the London playhouses were just starting up; but the expanding market must have looked a bright prospect for a young poet in 1576, when the 22-year-old Stephen Gosson left Oxford.

Over the next thirty years, commercial theatre became more firmly established as part of the capital's entertainment scene, while its connections with authority grew more sophisticated and more centralized. By the 1590s, every play-script had to be submitted for licensing and possible censorship by the officer responsible for selecting the plays performed at court, the Master of the Revels. Meanwhile the principal London companies gravitated towards the patronage of the crown and a handful of the most senior courtiers. The aristocracy was never the theatre's most numerically dominant audience constituency, though the financial rewards for court performances could be considerable; but association with the very top of the establishment provided drama with a modicum of security in the face of its zealous enemies, at least until those political structures were swept away when the English Revolution came in 1642. Individual playhouses and companies came and went, but for more than sixty years there was a more or less regular demand for new plays to be written.

Shakespeare spent his entire career as an actor-dramatist in this commercial sector of the drama industry; but many of his contemporaries also worked for another kind of theatre, which had its origins in a tradition of amateur performance, and which was establishing itself inside the city walls at the same time as the professional players were setting themselves up among the bawdy-houses of London's northern fringe. In 1575, Sebastian Westcott, the recusant master of the choir school attached to St Paul's Cathedral, began to admit paying audiences to performances given by his boys in an indoor playhouse within the cathedral precincts. The city's other important group of choristers, from the Chapel Royal, followed suit in 1576 when their deputy master, Richard Farrant, took out a lease on a property in the up-market Blackfriars district and had it converted into a theatre. This was the 'respectable' face of the mid-1570s theatre boom: performing weekly rather than daily like their adult counterparts, the boy companies catered for more exclusive audiences and charged higher admission prices. They also had a far more chequered career, winking in and out of existence several times before they were finally absorbed into the milieu of adult commercial theatre in the early seventeenth century.

Today the idea of choirboys performing in public for the enrichment of their masters seems distasteful. (It didn't pass without comment at the time, either.) Although it eventually became an unashamedly profit-making enterprise, however, it began as part of an educational movement. The schools and universities were the other great estate of English drama in the sixteenth century: amateur performances, in Latin, Greek, and the vernacular, were a regular feature of academic life. The trend was initiated in late *quattrocento* Italy, with productions of the classical plays which were part of the university curriculum; and in England, new plays soon began to appear alongside the works of Seneca and Terence. The dramatists were often quite senior dons— college fellows, university proctors, and even two successive bursars of Queens' College, Cambridge, Nicholas Robinson and John Mey— and amateur acting was considered part of a student's course of study. Although one purpose was simply 'to recreate ourselves . . . with some learned poem or other', as the Oxford playwright William Gager put it, they also made a contribution to the undergraduates' study of rhetoric, not only allowing them to practise oral delivery but also providing 'such domestical examples and precepts of well speaking, as, if many that dislike such exercises . . . had followed, so many sole-cisms in utterance should not be committed so often as there are'.[4]

Original school drama is first recorded at Magdalen College School, Oxford at the end of the fifteenth century, possibly during the brief tenure of Thomas More's friend, John Holt, as the school's Usher in 1494–5 (More himself may have helped to write some of the scripts); during the next eighty years or so, plays were encouraged, and sometimes written, by visionary headmasters such as Nicholas Udall at Eton (*c.*1534–41) and Richard Mulcaster at Merchant Taylors' (1561–86). As in the two universities, the purpose was to give the boys practical experience in rhetoric; and at the choir schools, where singing was an important part of the curriculum, the plays also had a strong musical content. But though education was academic drama's 'legitimate' end, recreation should not be underestimated. Udall argued as much in the prologue to his schoolboy comedy, *Ralph Roister Doister* (1552):

> mirth prolongeth life and causeth health,
> Mirth recreates our spirits and voideth pensiveness,
> Mirth increaseth amity, not hindering our wealth,
> Mirth is to be used both of more and less,
> Being mixed with virtue in decent comeliness,
> As we trust no good nature can gainsay the same;
> Which mirth we intend to use, avoiding all blame.

The universities would lay on productions for the 'mirth', in the word's broad sense of entertainment, of visiting dignitaries—one of Stephen Gosson's teachers at Oxford, John Rainolds, had worn skirts in front of the Queen as a teenage performer in *Palamon and Arcite* (1566, mostly lost), much to his later embarrassment when he became a dedicated opponent of stage transvestism—and when members of London's law schools, the Inns of Court, began staging comedies and tragedies in the 1560s, it was explicitly for 'mirth' as part of their Christmas celebrations. Like Peter Quince and his artisans in *A Midsummer Night's Dream*, moreover, amateur schoolboy actors were frequent contributors to the revels at court: they dominated early Elizabethan court theatre until Lent 1572, after which the death of the Queen's first Master of the Revels, Sir Thomas Benger, and the new patronage requirements for professional companies saw policy and taste shift towards adult players.

At this time a headmaster would receive an annual stipend of between £20 and £35. Performing at court offered a lucrative supplement: the Revels Office paid a fee of £6 13s. 4d. for each play, rising to £10 in 1576. It seems to have been Richard Mulcaster, not only the most distinguished schoolmaster of his generation but also one of the most underpaid, who first thought of extending the market by charging members of the public to see his Merchant Taylors' boys perform. In 1574, the school's governors, offended that no seats had been reserved for them, put a stop to the practice. The following year,

Westcott opened his playhouse at St Paul's, and the boy actors entered the commercial arena in earnest.

One reason for the companies' erratic history was that plays were only a sideline, which could be dropped if the profits were too small, or if the choirmasters lost interest. After Farrant and Westcott died, in 1580 and 1582 respectively, their successors had no theatrical inclinations, though they were happy to allow the would-be courtier John Lyly to run an amalgamated company drawing on boys from both Cathedral and Chapel. This troupe—whose repertory included Lyly's own comedies and, almost certainly, Christopher Marlowe's first play, *Dido, Queen of Carthage* (1586)—performed at Blackfriars until 1584, when they were evicted by a landlord who had expected his house to be used as a schoolroom rather than a theatre, and then from 1586 at the Paul's playhouse. In 1590 they split up into their two constituent parts, probably divided their playbooks between them, and toured the provinces for a year or two before disappearing altogether.

Because of its educational origins, choirboy theatre existed outside the licensing system which regulated the adult companies: the boys' output did not become subject to censorship by the Master of the Revels until 1606. It may have been exploiting this liberty which brought about the demise of Lyly's Paul's company—some scholars believe the playhouse was suppressed by the government after an outbreak of political satire—though it is also possible that it was simply edged out commercially by its adult competitors. In any event, when the boy companies were revived in 1599, a prominent part of their smart-set appeal lay in sexual licentiousness and political insolence, the former no doubt made the more piquant by the young mouths from which it issued. But if scandal made for good business in the short term, it also meant institutional instability: under heavy moral pressure from London's zealotry, Paul's playhouse closed for good in 1606, while persistent mockery of friendly foreign powers, Scottish courtiers, and even the King himself, led in 1608 to the temporary withdrawal of royal patronage from the Queen's Revels Boys (as the Chapel boys had become four years earlier). Once the boy companies were brought under the authority of the Master of the Revels, they ceased to be entirely distinct from the adult professionals: over the next few years the child actors grew up and, in Hamlet's phrase, 'grew to common players'.

The opponents of the stage usually did their best to keep common and academic players distinct from one another, admitting the educational case for drama whilst dismissing the recreational. Certainly the surviving university and Inns of Court plays, static, declamatory, and often in Latin, seem quite unsuitable for the paying audiences of the capital: with much of the action relegated from the stage while the characters swap lengthy speeches of disputation, they reflect the tastes, interests, and attention-spans of trainee lawyers and scholars rather than the common playgoer; and in practice, their very brief theatrical lives lasted a mere handful of performances—often only one. The best of them, however, went on to a second life in print or circulated manuscript as texts for reading; some became much respected literary works, such as Thomas Sackville and Thomas Norton's Inns of Court tragedy *Gorboduc* (1562) and the Latin trilogies *Richard III* (1580) and *The Destruction of Jerusalem* (1584) by Thomas Legge, the Master of Gonville and Caius College and sometime Regius Professor of Civil Law at Cambridge.

The London boy companies retained something of the literary and intellectual cachet of their academic roots even in the second, more commercial phase of their existence. After a slow start in 1599 when Paul's had to pad out its repertory with revivals that were scorned as 'musty fopperies of antiquity', the boys attracted a range of established literary figures to be their scriptwriters: the verse satirist John Marston, the sonneteer Samuel Daniel, and George Chapman, the poet and future translator of Homer; Ben Jonson too had literary ambitions as yet unfulfilled.[5] These dramatists seem not only to have retained a measure of control over their scripts but also to have published them like their academic counterparts: nearly half the surviving commercial-theatre plays written during the ten years between 1599 and 1608 were originally performed by boys, a very considerable proportion of their repertory given that they acted only once a week and consequently must have bought fewer new plays than the adult companies. In contrast, playwrights like Shakespeare who worked mainly or exclusively for the adults usually gave up rights in their work, and in some cases were actively hostile to publication, seeing drama as an art form that worked through performance rather than private reading.

However, it is all too easy to overemphasize the differences between the various institutions producing drama, at the expense of the associations between them. The gradual professionalization of the boy companies cut across the clear demarcation which the antitheatrical-ists wanted to maintain between the academic and the commercial stage, and by 1600 the adult actors certainly saw them as competitors. None of these groups worked in isolation from the others. The common players relied on the universities for the literate, intelligent young men who most often wrote their plays: Stephen Gosson's move from study at Oxford to play-writing in London is paradigmatic of many a later career—John Lyly and Christopher Marlowe, Robert Greene and Thomas Middleton were all graduate dramatists. In turn, many of the scriptwriters who migrated to the boy companies when they reopened, such as Jonson, Chapman, and Marston, already had professional experience with the adults. Finally, Oxford alumni work-ing in the London theatre would occasionally return to help out their *alma mater* with productions: the 1566 *Palamon and Arcite* was written by the former Christ Church don Richard Edwards, by then the choirmaster in charge of the Chapel boys, and in 1583 the dramatist George Peele, also of Christ Church, came back to his old college to produce two of William Gager's Latin plays. These were not institu-tions so utterly distinct that human resources could not circulate among them.

Moreover, university and playhouse audiences were not so entirely segregated, in taste or even in person, as antitheatrical opinion might have assumed. University-written drama may have observed due clas-sical decorum, but Oxford students also sometimes revived plays that had first been seen on London stages; some plays in the boys' reper-tories seem to have been written for, or at least with an eye on, the common players' amphitheatres and inn-yards, with characters issuing warnings against cutpurses who can hardly have been much of a danger to the seated audiences at the indoor playhouses; and Shake-speare's company, pre-eminent among the adults, performed not only for their regular London clientele but also, on occasion, at Inns of Court revels; all three groups entertained the Queen many times. The modes of scriptwriting may sometimes have been different, and the playgoers socially and intellectually variegated, but student amateurs, choirboy actors, and adult professionals were all ultimately engaged in the same activity, the production of plays whose common aim was to please an audience which evidently had some continuity of taste.

The Matter of Plays

Given that, at the simplest level, a play would please by telling a story, what playwrights needed most of all after the late 1570s boom in demand was a plenteous supply of fresh plots. In a period when plays were more often adapted from existing narratives than invented anew, the main supplier was the printing press: the availability for the first time of relatively cheap, mass-produced books created an information explosion in the sixteenth century which provided its dramatists with extensive raw material. 'I may boldly say it because I have seen it,' avers Gosson, 'that *The Palace of Pleasure*, *The Golden Ass*, *The Ethiopian History*, *Amadis of France*, the round table, bawdy comedies in Latin, French, Italian, and Spanish, have been thoroughly ransacked to furnish the playhouses in London.'[6]

It is hard to give a precise and comprehensive account of the relationship between dramatic and non-dramatic Elizabethan fiction. The existing evidence is sometimes easy to interpret, and tends to confirm Gosson's remarks: we know that Anthony Munday's *Fedele and Fortunio* (1583–4) was based on a not especially bawdy Italian comedy printed at Venice in 1576, and we may reasonably infer that the anonymous *Chariclea* (1572, lost) took its title character, and presumably its plot, from Heliodorus' Greek romance *Aethiopica* (translated 1569); similarly, the Paul's play *Cupid and Psyche* (anonymous, 1581, lost) must have been based on the central story of Apuleius' *Golden Ass* (translated 1566), which also supplied elements of Peele's *The Arraignment of Paris* (also 1581). But all too often, the scanty surviving information is obscure: nobody has ever identified the Italian material on which Gosson said he based his *Captain Mario*, for example, so we can only conjecture that the play might have been about the kind of braggart soldier popular in Italian Renaissance comedy. Many titles do not allow even this kind of informed guesswork.

Even so, it is possible to generalize that the stage followed developing tastes in leisure reading. In practice this meant a diversification of genre. Up to the middle of the century, chivalric romances like the stories of King Arthur's knights of the round table or the Spanish romance *Amadis of Gaul* (translated 1567) were the dominant narrative form in print. Such tales had been a part of the dramatic repertory since the middle of the fifteenth century, and they were still popular in the late 1570s, when audiences were offered plays (all anonymous, and all lost) like *The Red Knight, The Solitary Knight, The Irish Knight*, and *The Knight in the Burning Rock*; typically these would have shown what Gosson describes as 'the adventures of an amorous knight, passing from country to country for the love of his lady, encountering many a terrible monster made of brown paper, and at his return is so wonderfully changed that he cannot be known but by some posy in his tablet, or by a broken ring, or a handkercher, or a piece of a cockleshell'.[7] However, new kinds of fiction were emerging: knights and maidens now shared the bookseller's stall, and the stage, with courtly amours, classical Mediterranean adventures, and modern Italianate intrigue. Most important of all, as Gosson indicates in his account of the satanic origins of England's recent literary history, was the Italian novella.

The sensational modern short stories of Matteo Bandello and others began to reach England in the 1560s, shocking conservative readers with their racy portrayals of vindictiveness, cruelty, and promiscuity. Plays began to draw on Italian themes early in the decade (including, in about 1561, a dramatization of the Romeo and Juliet story), and the genre took off when collections of novellas began to appear in English translation. For playwrights, the value of such collections was partly in the number of tales they contained: a compendium would obviously stretch further than a single work. The largest and longest-serving was William Painter's *The Palace of Pleasure* (1566–7): it was probably the source of the plays about Gismond of Salerno and Cyrus and Panthea for which Richard Farrant wrote songs in the late 1570s (only the songs survive), and dramatists were still selecting material from its 101 stories well into the next century, notably for the plots of Shakespeare's *All's Well That Ends Well* (1605) and Webster's *The Duchess of Malfi*.

'Traffic [trade] and travel have woven the nature of all nations into ours', remarked John Lyly in the prologue to *Midas* (1589); and the developing pluralism of English culture in the sixteenth century was reflected in playwrights' treatment not only of fiction but also the considerable body of factual and pseudo-factual material supplied by the press. It was in this period that the two more or less incompatible traditions, the classical and the Christian, of which Western civilization is the uneasy inheritor, began to compete for dominance. Classical texts became central to the educational curriculum after the humanist reforms early in the century, forming an authoritative corpus of historical and mythological narrative which stood in apposition to the two great bodies of Christian story, the Bible and the lives of the saints. Although this nominally extended the range of potential source material, however, in practice there was simply a marked shift of emphasis across the century, away from Christian topics and towards classical ones.

Ironically it was the godly themselves who most contributed to the decline of Christian theatre, and the consequent proliferation of secular themes. Plays about saints' lives had disappeared by the 1540s, frowned upon after the Reformation; but biblical plays presented a more complex issue. While Protestantism swept away the saints as mere popish superstition, the Bible acquired even greater authority now that it was the only recognized source of divine revelation. This meant, however, that it was no longer regarded as a source of holy material which could usefully be translated into other media, such as drama, for the enlightenment of the illiterate; on the contrary, it had become important as a written text in its own right. Moreover, Protestant suspicion of the image made Reformation divines the natural enemies of the theatre. During the 1570s, local authorities suppressed the old medieval mystery play cycles, performed on Corpus Christi day by a town's craft guilds and dramatizing biblical events from Creation to Doomsday; and at the same time biblical topics came to feature less and less among the offerings of the professional companies.

Such plays were not extinct by Shakespeare's time, but they were not an especially prominent element in the range: only two survive— *David and Bathsheba* (Peele, 1587) and *A Looking-Glass for London and England* (Lodge and Greene, 1588), the latter dealing with Jonah and the fall of Nineveh—along with a handful of titles, nearly half of them from the single year 1602, when evidently they were briefly in fashion. What is striking is the predominance of Old Testament subjects, and in particular the most secular, most political parts of the Bible, the books from Joshua to Kings chronicling the formation and zenith of the Israelite nation: among the 1602 plays were *Jephthah* (by Thomas Dekker and Anthony Munday), *Joshua* (by Samuel

Rowley), *Absalom*, and *Samson* (both anonymous). One reason for this must have been concern about the potential blasphemy of representing God on stage, whether as Father or Son, and the risk of consequent prosecution; the sole New Testament plays, *Pontius Pilate* (anonymous, 1597, lost) and *Judas* (Bird and Rowley, 1601, lost), dealt with key figures in the crucifixion story but probably kept Jesus off stage, much as history plays like *Sir Thomas More* (Munday and others, 1595) and *Thomas, Lord Cromwell* (anonymous, 1600) avoided representing Henry VIII in person during the Queen his daughter's lifetime. It is possible, too, that Bible stories were simply considered down-market. The one form of drama in which they remained current and popular throughout the period was the most demotic, the 'motion' or puppet-show, which offered fairground audiences such themes as the Creation, the destruction of Nineveh, and, most surprisingly, the Resurrection, acted out by glove puppets with the dialogue delivered in the squeaky, nasal style familiar from Punch and Judy today.

Classical themes did not feature greatly in the repertoire of the puppeteers—when Ben Jonson parodied their 'motions' in *Bartholomew Fair* (1614), he wryly transferred the Hero and Leander story from ancient Sestos to contemporary London, 'to reduce it to a more familiar strain for our people' (5. 3. 116–17)—but everywhere else they burgeoned as the sixteenth century went on. The principal areas of interest were mythology and Roman history: the Trojan War and its aftermath was an especial favourite, and though Roman plays ranged widely from the last days of the Tarquins in *The Rape of Lucrece* (Heywood, 1607) to the dissolute later emperors in *Heliogabalus* (anonymous, 1594, lost) and *Valentinian* (Fletcher, 1614), the greatest concentration of attention was on the middle to late republic, and in particular on the Punic Wars, the conspiracy of Catiline, and the career of Julius Caesar, the single most dramatized historical figure in the English Renaissance. Unsurprisingly, these were also the subjects covered by the three Latin historians most often studied in the Elizabethan grammar schools, Livy, Sallust, and Caesar; and while the playwrights generally did not use these school texts as sources (Appian's *Roman History* and Plutarch's *Lives*, translated in 1578 and 1579 respectively, were the commonest suppliers of raw material), the familiarity of the events and characters must have been a key factor in the selection of subject matter.

No matter how much Latin an Elizabethan schoolboy may have known, he would always have had less Greek. The history of the other great classical civilization was rarely dramatized outside the universities, and then mainly in plays dealing with semi-legendary figures, such as *Timoclea* (anonymous, 1574, lost), *Campaspe* (Lyly, 1583), and *Timon of Athens* (Shakespeare, 1607). The material was available to dramatists—Plutarch's *Lives* covered the Greeks as well as the Romans—but they evidently chose not to use it. Classical plays, like biblical ones, dealt with events and characters which, whether perceived as historical or fictitious, were part of their audience's common cultural knowledge. The Troy story fascinated partly because it ended with the beginning of Roman history, as recounted in Virgil's *Aeneid*, another schoolroom perennial and the ultimate source of many a play on the Dido and Aeneas story; but also because England's legendary history credited another Trojan refugee, King Brutus, with the foundation of London. In contrast, what the Greeks did next, or indeed ever again, was relatively obscure to all but the most highly educated: the best-known Pericles in English popular culture was not the great Athenian statesman but the Prince of Tyre in Shakespeare's play (1607).

Dramatists' choices of factual topic, then, were determined by a broad sense of the common cultural identity which they shared with their audience. In Stephen Gosson's time that culture was still defined, however remotely, by the pan-European ideals of the Renaissance humanists: the English were among the Christian inheritors of ancient Rome, the more so because of their shared Trojan ancestry; so naturally their historical drama was biblical, Roman, and Trojan in its concerns. A more specific Englishness, in so far as it was represented on the stage at all, was limited to farces with native settings such as *Gammer Gurton's Needle* (W. Stevenson, 1553). The century's great revolution in subject matter was the emergence of the English history play during the 1580s.

There had been occasional forays into post-classical history before then—John Bale had used the reign of King John for a two-part Protestant propaganda play in 1538, and in 1580 Dr Legge's students at Cambridge had presented his *Richard III* trilogy—but it was not until *The Famous Victories of Henry V* (anonymous, 1586–7) that the professional theatre began to draw themes from this area. Thereafter

English historical subjects became extraordinarily popular, and the genre received a great boost by the publication in 1587 of the second edition of Raphael Holinshed's *Chronicles*, which resourced more surviving plays than any other book; by the end of the 1590s 'histories' had entered the dramatic trinity alongside tragedies and comedies, supplanting 'morals', which had been the recognized third genre in Gosson's day. With the conspicuous exception of Roman Britain, the later Elizabethan stage represented every era from King Brutus to the Tudors, with especial attention to the century from Richard II to Richard III, the latter the most dramatized English king of all.

With English history as with Roman, drama retold stories which playgoers already knew to some extent. In fact, the usurpation of Richard III was so familiar that several plays were written with the expectation that audiences could fill in for themselves parts of the story that were not represented on stage. For instance, *The True Tragedy of Richard III* (anonymous, 1591; not to be confused with Shakespeare's play) diminishes the stage time spent on Richard and his scheming, arguably the central events of the narrative, in order to concentrate instead on how it affects his subjects; and in the final scene of *Edward IV, Part 2* (anonymous, but sometimes attributed to Heywood, 1599), the contemptuous complacency with which the newly crowned Richard dismisses Buckingham when he defects to Richmond— 'What, is he gone in heat? Why, farewell he. | He is displeased; let him be pleased again. | We have no time to think on angry men.' (Z2^r)—is heavily ironized by an entirely unprompted audience foreknowledge of Richmond's part in future events beyond the scope of this particular play. Again, historical themes are drawn from a shared past which defines cultural identity; but by the mid-1580s, as war loomed with the Roman Catholic powers on the Continent, it had become a specifically national identity. No wonder playwrights avoided the subject of the Roman conquest: occupation by a foreign power, and in particular by Rome, can hardly have been a welcome theme at such a time.

Part of the appeal of all these historical plays, biblical, classical, and English, lay in the educated Renaissance fantasy of seeing the worthies of the past newly embodied as if they lived again. Marlowe's Doctor Faustus has devils to conjure up Helen of Troy for him, but playgoers had to make do with actors: 'It is no legend-lie,' declared the prologue to *Damon and Pithias* (Edwards, 1564), 'But a thing once done indeed, as histories do descry [show], | Which, done of yore in long time past, yet present shall be here | Even as it were in doing now, so lively [lifelike] shall it appear.' It should not be entirely surprising that Fabian Fitzdottrel, the fatuous hero of Ben Jonson's *The Devil is an Ass* (1616), has learned his history from plays because he thinks them more authentic than the chronicles: drama actually showed the people and exploits which history books could only report. Moreover, by the 1590s the stage was offering yet another kind of history play whose purpose was indeed, at one level, to inform in the way that Fitzdottrel assumes: the history of other European nations like France, the Netherlands, or Scotland. The last of these was a particular object of curiosity once it had become obvious, in the final years of the century, that its king, James VI, would be Queen Elizabeth's successor: dramatists quarried Scottish history in plays like *Robert II* (Jonson, Chettle, and Dekker, 1599, lost) and *Malcolm* (Charles Massey, 1602, lost), in order to satisfy a desire to learn about the background of the future James I of England, creating a minor genre which was eventually to produce *Macbeth* (Shakespeare, 1606).

There was one significant difference between foreign and English histories: except for notorious contemporary murders, English themes stopped mid-century with the brief reign of Lady Jane Grey, dramatized in 1602, until the accession of James made the Elizabethan past available in *The Troubles of Queen Elizabeth* (Heywood, 1604); but playwrights had no difficulty in dealing with recent events overseas. Plays like *The Massacre at Paris* (Marlowe, *c.*1591), the four-part *Civil Wars of France* (Drayton and Dekker, 1598–9, all lost), and *A Larum for London* (anonymous, 1599), about the sack of Antwerp, all handled near-contemporary political and religious affairs in Europe, whereas comparable English topics would simply not have been allowed by the censor. For playgoers, part of the interest would have lain in the very novelty of the material, in contrast with other histories' revivification of the familiar. Thomas Platter, a Swiss traveller who attended several theatres when he visited London in 1599, wrote of audiences 'learning at the play what is happening abroad . . . since the English for the most part do not travel much, but prefer to learn foreign matters . . . at home', and there was indeed an element of news reporting in some plays: for example, the fall of the Dutch statesman Sir John van

Oldenbarnevelt was being re-enacted on the London stage only months after his execution in May 1619.[8]

So the raw material for plays ranged from the far distant past to the virtually contemporary, and across the entire gamut of fiction. It was important for the narrative and generic scope of drama to open out from the 1570s onwards, because variety was in itself a recognized commercial imperative. When personifications of the three principal dramatic genres contend for possession of the stage in the induction to *A Warning for Fair Women*, Comedy says of Tragedy,

> she may for a day,
> Or two perhaps, be had in some request;
> But once in a week if we do not appear
> She shall find few that will attend her here.
>
> (35–8)

The point was true not only of the fundamental types of theatrical experience—laughter or tears—but also of the events that were represented: regular audiences would not pay to see endless variations on the same story. Without the copiousness of narrative material and the broadening of popular literary taste created by the new communications technology of the printing-press, the London playhouses might well have been a short-lived enterprise, closed down for lack of profits long before Marlowe and Shakespeare arrived in the capital in search of a career.

The Purpose of Playing

At the first climax of Thomas Heywood's tragedy, *A Woman Killed with Kindness* (1603), Anne Frankford, caught by her husband in the act of adultery and left alone on stage to await his reprisals, breaks off a soliloquy of anguished repentance to address a section of the audience directly:

> O women, women, you that have yet kept
> Your holy matrimonial vow unstained,
> Make me your instance: when you tread awry,
> Your sins, like mine, will on your conscience lie.
>
> (13. 141–4)

In these lines she steps outside the particularity of her circumstances and universalizes herself as an exemplary figure: the play is understood not just as a representation of certain individuals and their story, but also as something to be applied to corresponding situations in the lives of its audience. Anne the psychologically tormented penitent is, beyond herself, a terrible warning of the emotional consequences of adultery. In this instance, one of the purposes of playing is evidently to keep women in awe.

The emphasis on a play's thematic as well as its narrative content reflects one of the long-standing aesthetic assumptions of Western culture. Works of art are typically valued not for their own sake but according to their effects: the examples they set and the lessons they teach, the attitudes they support and the cultural and political developments they influence. The classical author Horace, whose *Art of Poetry* was familiar schoolroom reading for educated Elizabethans, argued influentially that the end of literature is either to profit or delight. His sixteenth-century successors usually expected plays to do both: their function was 'partly to delight, partly to move us to embrace examples of virtue and goodness, and to eschew vice and filthy living'; delight alone was not usually considered sufficient. Comedy was understood to be an admonitory representation of human error—'the promptness of youth unto vice, the snares of harlots and bawds laid for young minds, the deceit of servants'— whose purpose was dissuasion. Tragedy, meanwhile, dealt with the abuse of power—'the ulcers that are covered with tissue' (fine cloth)— in order to make 'kings fear to be tyrants', to move common men to 'pity and detestation', and 'to show the mutability of fortune, and the just punishment of God in revenge of a vicious and evil life'.[9] A minority defended delight in utilitarian terms as a valuable end in itself, but for most Renaissance literary theorists it was just a way of sugaring the pill; what mattered was drama's profitable lessons in ethical and political virtue.

Playwrights, particularly those recruited from the universities, cannot have been unaware of these concepts of literariness, and those few who spoke about their art in general terms emphasized the social usefulness of its effect on the audience. Occasionally this might involve the direct application of events on stage to real life: it was rumoured that plays had sometimes terrified criminals into confession by representing the image of their crimes before them, the principle Hamlet hopes to use against Claudius in staging *The Murder of Gonzago* at court. More often, inevitably, any application was bound to be indirect. Gosson describes the aims of his tragedy, *Catiline's Conspiracies* (*c.*1578, lost), which dealt with the events of 63 BC when the consul Cicero exposed a plot to overthrow the Roman state, almost entirely in abstract terms: 'the whole mark [target] which I shot at in that work was to show the reward of traitors in Catiline, and the necessary government of learned men in the person of Cicero, which foresees every danger that is likely to happen and forestalls it continually ere it take effect.'[10] What he sought to 'show' the audience, that is, was the fall not of Catiline but of all men like Catiline: plot and character, which today we tend to consider the fundamental elements of a play, were for Gosson only vehicles for making general, universally applicable points.

Most London playgoers, however, were more actively interested in the pleasures of the stage than its potential for moral instruction: the companies tempted them with titles promising plays that were *As Merry as May Be*, *As You Like It*, or *What You Will*, or, less blatantly, associating them with popular festivals like *May Day*, *All Fools*, and *Twelfth Night*, when workaday concerns were temporarily put aside. Although the Blackfriars boys were still offering 'morals' in their repertory as late as 1601, the old third genre was becoming uncommercial: 'The people make no estimation | Of morals teaching education,' commented Robert Greene in 1592.[11] It seems that audiences were not coming to the playhouses to be instructed but to be entertained.

However, there is also evidence, not least the words of Anne Frankford, to support an entirely opposite generalization. If playgoers like Jonson's Fitzdottrel were scorned for thinking they might learn something at the theatre, there was no less disdain for those who came merely 'to laugh and feed fool-fat' (1. 1. 323), as one of Chapman's characters puts it in *The Revenge of Bussy D'Ambois* (1610). Some titles, such as *A Warning for Fair Women*, drew attention to their plays' admonitory lessons, while others offered practical demonstrations of useful skills like *How to Learn of a Woman to Woo*, or *How a Man May Choose a Good Wife from a Bad*. A few audience members even crystallized their theatregoing experiences into maxims like 'Beware of trusting feigned beggars and fawning fellows', as the astrologer Simon Forman advised himself after seeing the confidence trickster Autolycus in *The Winter's Tale* (*c*.1610).[12]

In short, it is impossible to place the commercial theatre exclusively on one side of the issue or the other: the Horatian axis between education and entertainment ran deep. However, the last quarter of the sixteenth century saw a significant change in the balance, which can be illustrated by juxtaposing the way two plays, written respectively before and after the establishment of the permanent London theatres, introduce themselves in their prologues. The anonymous chivalric romance, *Clyomon and Clamydes* (*c*.1570), begins with an unspecific account of the subject matter and its literary origins, but is more precise about the play's themes and moral purpose:

> Our author he hath found the glass of glory shining bright,
> Wherein their lives are to be seen which honour did delight,
> To be a lantern unto those which daily do desire
> Apollo's garland by desert in time for to aspire;
> Wherein the froward chances oft of Fortune you shall see;
> Wherein the cheerful countenance of good successes be;
> Wherein true lovers findeth joy, with hugy heaps of care;
> Wherein as well as famous facts [deeds], ignomious placèd are;
> Wherein the just reward of both is manifestly shown
> That virtue from the root of vice might openly be known [differentiated].

The audience is told to interpret the ensuing story as an illustration of commonplace ideas about fortune, virtue, and vice; the story itself is deemed so insignificant that it is described in only the most general terms. It is an opening address which could fit almost any play of the same genre and period. The prologue of Marlowe's *Doctor Faustus* (*c*.1588), in contrast, recounts in some detail the life of the play's doomed academic hero:

> Now is he born, his parents base of stock,
> In Germany, within a town called Rode.
> Of riper years to Wittenberg he went,
> Whereas his kinsmen chiefly brought him up.
> So soon he profits in divinity,
> The fruitful plot of scholarism graced,
> That shortly he was graced with doctor's name.

Here there is a sense that the plot and the central character matter in themselves, that they are not just there to be instantly translated into some platitudinous aphorism about the hazards of ambition and curiosity. It is only after we have seen Faustus carried off to hell that the play opens itself out to generalization in its closing lines:

> Faustus is gone. Regard his hellish fall,
> Whose fiendful fortune may exhort the wise
> Only to wonder at unlawful things
> Whose deepness doth entice such forward wits
> To practise more than heavenly power permits.

In the twenty-odd years between the two plays, drama evidently became far more conscious of the inherent pleasures of fiction and narrative, and this changed the way in which it encouraged audiences to apply that narrative. Though only a few of its characters explicitly personify abstract concepts, *Clyomon and Clamydes* is virtually a simple allegory, because it emphasizes its general concerns before it begins to tell the tale. *Doctor Faustus*, however, works—or at least purports to work—as an exemplary story whose individual distinctiveness reinforces the awful warning with which it ends: the more the audience is engaged with Faustus as a character, the more appalled and apprehensive it will be at his ultimate fate.

One reason for this shift of emphasis must have been the changes in playhouse institutions during the period. With drama no longer a rare treat performed for a short run by itinerant actors, but a permanently available commodity offered by several competitors, theatre became a buyer's market; the profit-and-delight balance was bound to tip somewhat towards delight. Moreover, the need to offer variety in subject matter would have led dramatists and companies to emphasize the things that differentiated their plays from one another; and whereas there are many different situations and characters, the abstract concepts that interest any particular culture at any one time are relatively few. It is no wonder that these years saw the decline of the morality play: the appeal of yet another disquisition on fortune's mutability or the inevitable punishment of vice must have been negligible compared with the temptations of an afternoon with Julius Caesar, or Richard III, or Tamburlaine.

For all its concern to entertain its audience, however, the drama of Shakespeare's time never entirely discarded its concern with transferable wisdom, whether of ethical or pragmatic application. Some characters had a dual existence, both as agents and commentators, both living their own lives and transforming them into sententious aphorisms for the audience to take away, sometimes with the crude directness of Anne Frankford's warning to wives, sometimes with the stark simplicity of King Henry IV's 'Uneasy lies the head that wears a crown' (*Henry IV, Part 2*, 3. 1. 31). It was not hard to satirize playgoers who used drama as a literal source of practical advice, like the non-Shakespearian version of Christopher Sly in *The Taming of a Shrew* (anonymous, *c.*1593; probably an imitation of Shakespeare's play), who goes home thinking he has learnt how to tame his own wife. But a tendency to draw the general out of the particular was nonetheless one of the period's fundamental habits of interpreting narrative, too deeprooted to be ignored: the theorists' attention to the moral profitability of literature was never just an abstruse academic fancy irrelevant to the actual business of writing plays.

This is why it was so easy for a serious-minded young playwright like Stephen Gosson to turn so spectacularly against the art which had sustained him. If every story was also a lesson, then the lessons of drama could be bad ones as well as good:

how to ravish [rape]; how to beguile; how to betray, to flatter, lie, swear, forswear; how to allure to whoredom; how to murder; how to poison; how to disobey and rebel against princes, to consume treasures prodigally, to move to lusts, to ransack and spoil cities and towns, to be idle, to blaspheme, to sing filthy songs of love, to speak filthily, to be proud; how to mock, scoff, and deride any nation.

It was the same principle which led Gosson first to write his play showing how traitors come to a bad end, and then to denounce plays in general for the evil they taught. He went on to live through the entire golden age of English drama to whose early development he had contributed; he died just a few months after the appearance of the first collected edition of Shakespeare's plays. Even if the ageing clergyman was aware of the extent of their artistic achievement, he cannot have felt any pride in the small part he had once played in making it possible. In his last word on the subject, published more than forty years before, he had declared, 'Plays are the inventions of the devil, the offerings of idolatry, the pomp of worldlings, the blossoms of vanity, the root of apostasy, the food of iniquity, riot, and adultery: detest them.'[13] Fortunately not everyone did.

2

New Tragedies for Old

'Modern drama' began late for the Elizabethans. The time of Stephen Gosson may have bequeathed the theatrical institutions within which it took place, but it was not until the second half of the 1580s that the playhouses achieved their first durable popular successes, plays which not only defined audience taste for years afterwards, but were also individually memorable in their own right. The earliest to appear was probably Thomas Kyd's *The Spanish Tragedy* (*c.* 1586), which dealt with crime, politics, and imperialism in a fictitious modern court of Spain, the mightiest of the secular states of sixteenth-century Europe. *Tamburlaine the Great* soon followed in 1587, dramatizing the rise to power of a Tartar bandit turned would-be world conqueror; and its author, Christopher Marlowe, went on to co-write (with an unknown collaborator) another major success in *Doctor Faustus*, a tragic morality play in which, for once, the magic-fixated protagonist is not saved at the end but goes to hell. Conjuring Faustus, mighty Tamburlaine, and *The Spanish Tragedy*'s grieving, vengeful Hieronimo, were to become part of the period's common cultural discourse, as familiar in casual allusion as figures like Hercules and Aeneas, Adam and Jesus, from England's inherited mythologies.

These are plays on the cusp of a seismic shift in drama which was more or less complete by the time Shakespeare began his writing career in about 1590. In some respects they look back to the theatre of the recent past. This is most obvious in *Doctor Faustus*, which not only inhabits the conceptual world of the old allegorical drama but also uses many of its stage devices, like the Good and Evil Angels that prompt the devil-ridden hero towards sin and repentance. But *The*

Spanish Tragedy and *Tamburlaine the Great* too were inheritors of the age of Gosson, at least in their subject matter: Kyd was not the first English dramatist to write about murder and revenge, and the lost play *The Sultan* (anonymous, 1580) testifies to an interest in eastern potentates even before Marlowe made them a subject of fashionable fascination. Yet these were also plays which seemed to their first audiences so radically, excitingly new that they all but erased the memory of Stephen Gosson and his colleagues.

At the most superficial level, one reason for this sense of novelty was simply that the writing of Marlowe and Kyd *sounded* new. The plays of the late 1570s which their work displaced would seem comically crude to ears that are accustomed to the mellifluous dramatic verse of Shakespeare and his contemporaries. They were usually written in rhyming couplets, as Gosson avers: 'the poets send their verses to the stage upon such feet as continually are rolled up in rhyme at the fingers' ends, which is plausible [pleasing] to the barbarous'. A few were written in prose (Gosson mentions the exceptional case of 'two prose books [i.e. scripts] . . . where you shall find never a word without wit, never a line without pith, never a letter placed in vain'),[1] but the surviving texts show most playwrights using a hodge-podge of often irregular verse forms, especially 'fourteeners': 'I was so troubled in my mind with fright of sudden fear | That yet I feel my sinews shake and tremble everywhere.' (*Fedele and Fortunio*, 647–8) Less than four years after those lines were written, Marlowe sneeringly dismissed this sort of thing, in the prologue to *Tamburlaine the Great*, as 'jigging veins of rhyming mother wits'.

Though a skilful rhymer in his non-dramatic poetry, Marlowe wrote for the stage in blank verse, using stately, five-beat iambic pentameter lines like these from his first play, *Dido, Queen of Carthage*: 'Now, Dido, with these relics burn thyself, | And make Aeneas famous through the world | For perjury and slaughter of a queen.' (5. 1. 292–4) This was avant-garde writing when Lyly's boys first presented the play in 1586. For all Marlowe's condescension in *Tamburlaine*, rhymed fourteeners had, only five years before, been considered good enough for the standard Elizabethan translation of Seneca. Blank verse was a minority literary form, little used and less understood; yet its simplicity and economy made it an ideal medium for serious dramatic writing compared with the clunky over-elaboration that fourteeners can encourage. To the Elizabethans, Marlowe's plays must have had all the aural impact of a symphony orchestra taking over from a barrel-organ. And not only did this new verse form sound excellent, it also offered the ideal rhythm to suit the acoustic conditions of the London amphitheatres, as modern performances at the reconstructed Globe have shown. By the end of the 1580s, it had become the usual metre for plays, whatever their venue and audience: the lush referentiality of Marlowe's writing and the powerful emotion of Kyd's set a new standard of artful, thrilling rhetoric which other playwrights strove to rival; even Lyly, who had previously written his comedies exclusively in an polished, filigree prose, turned to blank verse for his last play, *The Woman in the Moon* (*c.*1592). The sound of drama had changed forever.

If their subject matter was old, moreover, Kyd and Marlowe breathed into it a new commercial life. The impact of *Tamburlaine the Great* in particular was immediate and awesome, and the first to exploit it was Marlowe himself: 'The general welcomes Tamburlaine received | When he arrivèd last upon our stage | Have made our poet pen his second part,' begins the prologue to the sequel, *The Second Part of Tamburlaine*, written only months after the original was first performed. A slew of lesser imitations followed, evoking the glamour of conquest in far-off lands, while others addressed the guilty fascination of magic, after *Doctor Faustus*, or the social, ethical, and political dilemmas of revenge, after *The Spanish Tragedy*; in the last years of its existence even Lyly's boy company, better suited to a less robust repertory, attempted to climb the conqueror bandwagon with *The Wars of Cyrus* (anonymous, 1588). Just as they had to learn to write in blank verse, older playwrights, left over from the London theatre's first decade, had to extend their range to satisfy the new fashions: George Peele, the Oxford dramatist who had begun his professional career writing witty pastorals for the boy actors, ended it with blood-and-thunder tragedy in the style of Christopher Marlowe.

Moral Ends and Amoral Endings

Beneath the shift of taste they generated, and beyond their technical innovations, Marlowe and Kyd were important for the new ethical and political sophistication of their plays, which initiated a fundamental artistic change in drama, and particularly in tragedy. Conventional justifications of the stage in the late sixteenth century, surveyed in the previous chapter, emphasized above all that it was politically safe. The purpose of drama was a moral one, it was asserted, and the morality was conservative: plays offered no challenge to the notions of degree and decorum which were central to Elizabethan social theory. On the contrary, they reinforced the existing order by showing the proper subordination of subject to ruler and the miserable end of traitors, and vindicated the inequalities of rank at all levels—placing old over young, master over servant, man over woman—by portraying members of the subjugated groups as errant, undisciplined figures in need of control by their superiors: youths were foolish and servants corrupt, and the warnings offered to fair women admonished them to obey their husbands and avoid adultery. In contrast, *The Spanish Tragedy*, *Tamburlaine the Great*, and *Doctor Faustus* all covered dangerous territory in their shared concern with the appropriation of power beyond the normal limits prescribed by society or by God, and their handling of the theme denied such stultifying moral simplicity.

Tamburlaine was the most obviously original play of the three, and the most intellectually perverse. Several elements of its imaginative appeal are evident in its poetic treatment of landscape, as in the words with which Tamburlaine woos his prisoner and future wife, the Egyptian princess Zenocrate:

> A hundred Tartars shall attend on thee,
> Mounted on steeds swifter than Pegasus;
> Thy garments shall be made of Median silk,
> Enchased with precious jewels of mine own,
> More rich and valurous than Zenocrate's;
> With milk-white harts upon an ivory sled
> Thou shalt be drawn amidst the frozen pools
> And scale the icy mountains' lofty tops,
> Which with thy beauty will be soon resolved [melted].

> (1. 2. 93–101)

This kind of soaring set-piece celebration of an unfamiliar environment, with its distinctive use of proper names and adjectives, was among the most imitable features of Marlowe's writing, and many another dramatist sought to reproduce the effect. Here is another wooing speech, from an anonymous comedy of the early 1590s, *The*

Taming of a Shrew (not to be confused with its Shakespearian cousin), which offers the same heady compound of classical allusion, exotic scenery, and glittering physical luxury:

> when I crossed the bubbling Canibey
> And sailed along the crystal Hellespont,
> I filled my coffers of the wealthy mines
> Where I did cause millions of labouring Moors
> To undermine the caverns of the earth
> To seek for strange and new-found precious stones
> And dive into the sea to gather pearl
> As fair as Juno offered Priam's son,
> And you shall take your liberal choice of all.

(4.74–82)

Both the weakness and the strength of the imitation can be seen in those millions of Moors: compared with Tamburlaine's hundred Tartars, the numerical exaggeration offers only crude overstatement; yet the playwright has also homed in astutely on another level of appeal beyond opulence and vicarious tourism. Just as Tamburlaine offers Zenocrate not only sight but ownership, so here the jewels of the earth are not only seen and enjoyed as part of a rich, exotic vista: they are mined. And in the image of Moors forced to slave in their millions to find them, we become uneasily aware of the fantasy's baser aspect.

In Marlowe's sequel, *The Second Part of Tamburlaine*, one of the subject kings, vassals and emulators of Tamburlaine himself, revealingly describes his adventures in Africa, which have included a trip to Zanzibar,

> The western part of Afric, where I viewed
> The Ethiopian sea, rivers, and lakes,
> But neither man nor child in all the land.
> Therefore I took my course to Manico.

(I. 3. 195–8)

This is no travelogue fired by the thrill of discovery: the new geography of the region seems incidental, and the absence of any population moves the explorer on. He conquers the rest of the dark continent; Zanzibar escapes only because there is not a human soul there for him to subjugate. It is relevant that some of the most memorable and most copied images in the two plays focus on acts of humiliation against defeated potentates: Bajazeth, once Emperor of the Turks, now confined to an iron cage and fed with scraps on the end of his master's sword, and, in the sequel, Tamburlaine's entrance onto the stage in a chariot drawn by conquered kings instead of horses. Both landscape and people are figured as things to be dominated, and the audience is imaginatively aligned with the hero who grasps so eagerly for dominion: part of the play's appeal is that of a fantasy of power.

Tamburlaine presents his ambition as a given fact: nature, he says, 'Doth teach us all to have aspiring minds' (2. 7. 20). This was the more challenging in coming from a protagonist of humble origins. Tamburlaine is a shepherd by birth and a bandit by inclination, but he refuses to accept the lowly status imposed in those roles: 'I am a lord, for so my deeds shall prove, | And yet a shepherd by my parentage.' (1. 2. 34–5) This must have been a startling assertion in 1587. An Elizabethan shepherd could not normally expect to become a gentleman, let alone a lord: the rigidly stratified society of contemporary orthodoxy was organized as an ascending hierarchy of allegiance and responsibility, culminating in the immense and centralized might of the crown; peasants and aristocrats each had their place and were expected to remain in it, their lofty or lowly status defining the nature of their actions. This is the principle by which Tamburlaine's enemies always calculate: they construe him as an ignorant peasant and his Tartar army as 'greedy-minded slaves' (2. 2. 67), who will, for instance, easily be distracted by treasure strategically scattered across the battlefield. In the event, however, his soldiers are not, as planned, cut to pieces while stooping for riches, and in consequence Tamburlaine wins his first major victory. The action consistently validates his position as he goes on to defeat progressively mightier opponents: his success comes through refusing to act true to type, through disdaining the base behaviour that is presumed to go with base birth; in that sense, his deeds do indeed prove his lordliness.

The plot of *Tamburlaine the Great*, showing the hero's ruthless ascent to power, has a simplicity which seems to be belied by the closing words of the prologue: 'View but his picture in this tragic glass | And then applaud his fortunes as you please.' Before the action begins, the audience is told the play's genre, tragedy, and its subject matter, Tamburlaine's fortunes. Tragedy, in the definition which the Elizabethans had inherited from the middle ages, dealt with the fall of great men, sometimes destroyed by the heavens in retribution for their overweening arrogance, and sometimes overthrown by the capricious and uncontrollable actions of Fortune: whether it emphasized the randomness of fate or the purposive working-out of providential history, it was a highly moral genre within the terms of contemporary dramatic criticism. So in its statement that the play is tragic, the prologue initiates an unseen context which ironizes the hero: Tamburlaine's career can be read as an exemplary illustration of pride, with the expectation that he will himself be the last of the story's great men to fall, his own fate foreshadowed in the treatment he metes out to his vanquished enemies. Such a conclusion would have enfolded the play safely back into contemporary social orthodoxy by showing the eventual punishment of excessive ambition. The play was most radically, shockingly new in withholding that expected moral ending: though his destruction is insistently telegraphed throughout, Tamburlaine finishes the play as the undefeated master of Asia. If the prologue seems to invite an interpretation according to the period's moralistic theories of drama, the conclusion calculatedly frustrates this—and the more you thought you knew about how tragedies worked, the more you would be wrong-footed by this one.

Marlowe faced several problems when box-office imperatives required a sequel. One was that he had already dramatized almost every significant element in the Tamburlaine story: all that was left was the conqueror's eventual demise. Accordingly the action is a long march to death, with the usual violence and victory *en route*. These elements were necessary because the appeal of commercially driven sequels is that they reproduce, with minor variations, the exciting experience of the original: audience demand traps their action within the parameters of the work which created that demand. That was the other problem: it might be easy enough to overturn the peaceful conclusion of *Tamburlaine the Great* and give playgoers the conquering hero they were paying to see, but the genre-shattering surprise of the first play's conclusion was obviously not directly reproducible; indeed, ending the sequel with the central character's death could all too easily reopen the whole story to the moralistic, exemplary reading so deliberately excluded from the available responses to the first play.

The Second Part of Tamburlaine is, accordingly, much more aggress-ive than its predecessor in unsettling the conventional moral positions which can inform an audience's casual reaction. Such pieties are exposed as mere expedient hypocrisy: the play's Christian characters are dishonourable and corrupt, anticipating Marlowe's fuller treat-ment of Christian perfidy in *The Jew of Malta* (1589); and though Tamburlaine's son refuses to fight on conscientious grounds—'I take no pleasure to be murderous' (4. 1. 29), he says—he is shown really to be just a coward and voluptuary. The conclusion builds on this dis-ruption by giving Tamburlaine a death that is temptingly legible as an act of nemesis: he burns a holy book, provocatively invites supernatural reprisals, and minutes later is struck by the sickness which kills him. Marlowe would have known from his studies at Cambridge the logical principle usually expressed in Latin as *post hoc non est propter hoc* (subsequently doesn't mean consequently), and in Tamburlaine's death he taunts the kind of literary interpretation which supposes otherwise; for the holy book the conqueror profanes is the Koran, and it is Muhammad whom he invites to take vengeance. Tamburlaine is guilty of sacrilege only in Islamic terms alien to playgoers who were Christian by law and habit even if not by zealous personal conviction, and so there can be no easy moral reading to guide the audience: it must, in the words of the previous play's prologue, applaud his fortunes as it pleases. It is the first attempt at an openness in the tragic conclusion which Marlowe was soon to push to its farthest extreme.

The Metaphysics of Calamity

The Spanish Tragedy can also look like a story of exciting human empowerment, albeit with a more reluctant hero than Tamburlaine. Its central character, Hieronimo, is presented as a victim of the unequal power relations in his society: he has no legal redress for his son's murder because, though he is himself a senior judge, the mur-derer, Lorenzo, is a member of the royal family, unassailable by public indictment; for him as later for Hamlet, the only available satisfaction is a private revenge. The narrative structure is accordingly very differ-ent from that of *Tamburlaine*, which develops through successive acts of military power constituting the stages of the ambitious hero's ascent to ultimate supremacy. The focus of Kyd's play is on a single, climactic act of destruction when Hieronimo irrevocably steps outside the law and takes a revenge that results in five deaths and destabilizes the kingdoms of Spain and Portugal by leaving them without an heir: the action leads towards a subordinate man's cataclysmic appropriation of power beyond his station.

What complicates this interpretation is the existence of another level to the action, continuously present but invisible to the characters: the main events are watched by an on-stage audience who 'serve for chorus' (1. 1. 91) and discuss the plot at the end of the play's acts. These are supernatural figures: the allegorical personification of Revenge has brought the ghost of Don Andrea to earth to witness the destruction of his killer, the Portuguese prince Balthazar. But what is perplexing, for the theatre audience as much as for the ghost, is that this declared plot seems not to match the actual events: the play seems more centrally concerned with the bereaved Hieronimo's vengeance than it is with Andrea's grievances, and Balthazar is at best a secondary character. Perhaps understandably, the ghost spends much of the entr'acte dialogue complaining that events are not following the course he expected, but diverting into a further, independent murder and its own separate revenge action. Revenge's consistent response is to demand patience—'Thou talkest of harvest when the corn is green' (2. 5. 7)—and ultimately the action does indeed reach the desired outcome: as one character says, 'The heavens are just, murder cannot be hid. | Time is the author both of truth and right.' (2. 4. 119–20) But the route by which that truth is revealed and that right achieved is obscure to human eyes, including those of the play's audience. Because Revenge lives in eternity, the whole action is already synoptically present to him as it cannot be to the human characters, including the ghost, who exist in time and can only see the events in sequence as they happen.

What Revenge necessarily underestimates is the temporary experience which, for him, is subsumed in the overall pattern: it is ironic that he should tell the ghost, 'imagine thou | What 'tis to be subject to destiny' (3. 15. 25–6), because that is precisely what he cannot imagine himself. Unlike *Tamburlaine*, whose hero proclaims his own mastery of fate—

> I hold the Fates bound fast in iron chains,
> And with my hand turn Fortune's wheel about,
> And sooner shall the sun fall from his sphere
> Than Tamburlaine be slain or overcome
>
> (1. 2. 174–7)

—the central dynamic of *The Spanish Tragedy* is human submission to fate. Its poetry also includes set-piece landscapes, but these are not, as in Marlowe, invigorating vistas, nor can they be possessed: they feature in narratives of a journey to hell, first told by Don Andrea (1. 1. 18–85) and later by Hieronimo (3. 13. 108–21), and their focus is on a human figure who is alienated and powerless in his uncanny environment. The central experience which the play dramatizes is the frustration and psychic suffering that arise from the characters' absolute dependence on mechanisms of justice which seem not to be operating. Hieronimo knows intellectually that he has two avenues of redress, first the King and then providence, and though his access to the former is blocked, he can still rely on the biblical assurance of God's justice:

> Ay, heaven will be revenged of every ill,
> Nor will they suffer murder unrepaid.
> Then stay, Hieronimo, attend their will,
> For mortal men may not appoint their time.
>
> (3.13.2–5)

Yet such patience is stressful beyond mortality's tolerance: it drives him over the edge into a madness which alienates him from his public identity as the state's principal executive officer of justice, but which also makes him, as a private revenger, the agent of a higher, supernatural justice. His vengeance destroys not only Lorenzo but Balthazar: it is the medium through which unseen powers have executed their very different purposes. The pity of it is that this process had, as it were, to go the long way round: it took a second murder to raise up an unwitting instrument of Don Andrea's revenge. The conclusion is just, with Revenge accompanying the ghost to the underworld, 'To place thy friends in ease, the rest in woes' (4. 5. 46); but we can never forget the cost of that justice in human pain and innocent life.

The Spanish Tragedy was the most widely quoted, copied, and, later, parodied play of its time. This material helps us to assess its impact on early audiences, because it shows which elements they found most memorable. Hieronimo figures largely, of course, but it is telling that he does not seem to have been associated with the Marlovian self-empowerment of his revenge: in fact, the most widely quoted of all his lines was the one with which he prudently restrains himself from overstepping the mark, 'Hieronimo, beware! Go by, go by!' (3. 12. 31) He seems to have been most compelling as an articulate but passive figure, a man to whom things are done: he was remembered as a character roused from sleep who demands, 'What outcries pluck me from my naked bed?' (2. 4. 63), just before discovering his dead son's body hanging in the garden, and who utters the manic poetry of grief—'O eyes, no eyes, but fountains fraught with tears' (3. 2. 1)—that Kyd's successors found so powerful and imitable. The central experience of the play for sixteenth-century audiences was his suffering.

Pain is an inevitable concomitant of tragedy, but in Kyd's play there is a distinct shift of emphasis from the genre's conventional tales of the fall of princes. Part of the response which such tragedies evoked was a grim, objective satisfaction at the humbling of the mighty, much as audiences tend to feel towards Tamburlaine's victims or the surviving royals at the end of *The Spanish Tragedy*. In contrast, the treatment of Hieronimo, a man of relatively lower rank, invites engagement and sympathy. Subsequent revenge plays followed suit: their heroes were known not as awesome angels of death sent to scourge the living, but for their almost insupportable burdens of human responsibility to the dead. It is no arbitrary chance that there survives from the first English tragedy based on the Hamlet story, written more than a decade before Shakespeare's version, only a single line of dialogue: it was the ghost's terrible injunction, 'Hamlet, revenge!' that playgoers most remembered and quoted.[2] Tragedy had begun to ask its audiences to respond with humane subjectivity; the essence of the experience was now a relationship with another human being.

This was as radical as *Tamburlaine the Great*'s refusal to supply the expected tragic catastrophe. If the genre's moral purpose was to show the mutability of fortune and the punishment of vice, then a degree of audience detachment was a necessary element: any pity which might be felt for the suffering hero served primarily to enhance the terror which made his destruction an effective moral example. In the new tragedy, the process was reversed: the terror of events now became the basis for pity, and this in turn made it impossible to represent the tragic outcome as transcendently right and just. Where conventional tragedy promoted an unquestioning acceptance of the order of things, these plays evoked a sense of regret that political and metaphysical circumstances should be such as to make suffering inevitable: as Shakespeare's Hamlet expresses it, 'The time is out of joint. O cursèd spite | That ever I was born to set it right!' (1. 5. 189–90) Often this works through a tension between our ethical sense of a moral ending and our humane sense of an unhappy ending. In *The Spanish Tragedy*, such feelings remain relatively unfocused; but in *Doctor Faustus* Marlowe and his collaborator made their object dangerously precise.

A play whose protagonist sells his soul, practises the forbidden arts of magic, and ends up damned cannot avoid the punitive dynamic: with angels and devils and, ultimately, the inescapable certainty of divine judgement, the action of *Doctor Faustus* literally depicts the Christian metaphysics which underpin and guarantee conventional moral thinking. Almost any seminar on the play will contain someone who wants to argue that the scholar hero gets his just deserts, and indeed when the discussion is framed in those terms it is difficult to disagree: the closing lines (quoted in the last chapter) expressly invite an exemplary reading of his 'hellish fall', and the action repeatedly emphasizes his more than suicidal folly. There is something ineluctably crass about a man who knows that the reward of sin is death, as it says in the biblical text that provokes him to reject theology, yet who chooses sin anyway; who declares that 'A sound magician is a mighty god' (1. 1. 64) when all his academic studies should have told him that there is a mightier; who conjures up the devil and then tells him that hell's a fable. Yet the epilogue also contains a simple, human statement which opens the play to a response beyond the merely judgemental: 'Faustus is gone.'

John Faustus is without doubt a failure. It is difficult to make a convincing case for a sense of tragic loss based on his appeal as a character, because that appeal lies more in desire than in act. There is a poetic magnificence in his initial fantasies about spirits that will fetch him gold from India and pearls from the deep, but they *remain* fantasies, unfulfilled even once he has the magical power to realize them: Germany is not given a defensive wall of brass, the university's poor students do not receive silken clothes, and he does not make himself the world's most powerful secular ruler. In his case, the waste of human potential has happened long before he goes to hell: though it is amusing and spectacular for him to give an insolent knight a pair of horns or fetch out-of-season fruit to satisfy a Duchess's pregnancy craving, such legerdemain is also imaginatively trivial.

It is important to recognize, however, that there is more than one kind of failure in the play. Faustus' greatest desire is for a knowledge that goes beyond the frustrating limits of the traditional academic disciplines, yet even with magic he learns nothing that he did not already know: his demonic factotum Mephistopheles will not, or cannot, enter into theological discussion, and when, in the revised version of the play produced nine years after Marlowe's death, Faustus explores the heavens to find out the secrets of astronomy, all he discovers are the enclosing concentric spheres of medieval cosmology which he could have read about in his own study. It is not Faustus' imagination that is at fault here, but the created world in which he exists: there is no new learning available to him because scholastic writers have told the truth about human existence, and he has already mastered their works. Both his folly and his desire spring from a conviction that there must be more to life than there really is: in a sense, he goes to hell because he is mistaken. This is the point at which we have to choose between orthodox and radical readings, between the old tragedy and the new. If the play reinforces conventional, conservative morality by condemning Faustus absolutely, then by implication it also condemns wishing for a better world. But if it does not condemn him, it must perforce call into question the world that is, and the presiding godhead that decrees damnation: if there is no justice, there can only be tyranny. It is sixteenth-century drama's most challenging dilemma.

The Lure of the Crown

Between them, Marlowe and Kyd reinvented tragedy for the English Renaissance, but of the three plays it was the least fundamentally tragic, *Tamburlaine the Great*, which exerted the most immediate and quantifiable influence. This extended well beyond the derivative and short-lived conqueror play genre: for nearly a decade afterwards, drama engaged widely with Marlowe's themes of ambition and social mobility. In the later 1590s, it was said that the typical story of a tragedy told 'How some damned tyrant, to obtain a crown, | Stabs, hangs, empoisons, smothers, cutteth throats.' (*A Warning for Fair Women*, induction, 50–1) Not the fall of princes now, but the rise of usurpers: aspirant characters like Shakespeare's Richard III and Marlowe's Duke of Guise in *The Massacre at Paris*, who are not born to supreme power but who seek it through crime and stratagem. If the insistent beat of that list of atrocities expresses severe criticism of the stage tyrant, the passage also evokes, in spite of itself, the new drama's tendency to depict the fascination of ambition as much as its hazards. The use of the word *crown* is distinctive, highlighted in end-stopped magnificence as the culmination not only of the usurper's aspirations but also of the pentameter line. This echoes the thrilling poetry of political desire first spoken by Tamburlaine:

> The thirst of reign and sweetness of a crown,
> That caused the eldest son of heavenly Ops
> To thrust his doting father from his chair
> And place himself in th' empyreal heaven
> Moved me to manage arms against thy state.

(2. 7. 12–16)

In the ensuing years, the crown was a subject of obsessive interest among stage villains: Stukely the ambitious Englishman can think of nothing else in *The Battle of Alcazar* (Peele, 1589), and in the anonymous *Edmond Ironside* (*c*.1592) the Machiavellian schemer Edricus even claims to value it above his own life. Shakespeare's reworking of Marlowe's lines, spoken by Richard of Gloucester in *Henry VI, Part 3* (1591), is especially interesting in the way it develops their mythological apparatus: 'How sweet a thing it is to wear a crown, | Within whose circuit is Elysium | And all that poets feign of bliss and joy.' (1. 2. 29–31) Tamburlaine, who cites the rise of Jove to the throne of the gods as an analogue for his own aspiration to an earthly crown, seems oddly respectful in comparison with Richard's assertion that bliss, the condition of the soul in heaven, is only a poetical fiction whose equivalent in reality is the satisfaction of kingship. This independence of supernatural sanction must have been shocking to early audiences; and it is an important part of the dynamic of ambition in these plays.

Richard's immediate problem as a would-be king is the existence of his elder brothers and their male issue, who stand between him and the throne according to the usual laws of succession. In *Richard III* (1592–3) he expresses this in terms of physical restriction: their deaths will 'leave the world for me to bustle in' (1. 1. 152), as if selective depopulation will give him more elbow-room. Atheism does much the same in existential terms. The title character of Robert Greene's Turkish conqueror play, *Selimus* (1592), who determines 'to arm myself with irreligion' (304), is even more explicit than Richard in his denial of hell: 'I think the cave of damnèd ghosts | Is but a tale to terrify young babes, | Like devil's faces scored on painted posts.' (424–6) Without the prospect of eternal punishment, there is no check on transgressive human action, and with no God there can be no purposeful providence but only the haphazard arbitrariness that a character in *Henry VI, Part 2* (1591) calls 'Fortune's pageant' (1. 2. 67). Moreover, if there is no higher power to which humanity is necessarily subject, a man can be the maker of his own destiny. Selimus articulates the point in metaphorically describing himself as a card-sharp:

> Will Fortune favour me yet once again,
> And will she thrust the cards into my hands?
> Well, if I chance but once to get the deck
> To deal about and shuffle as I would,
> Let Selim never see the daylight spring
> Unless I shuffle out myself a king.
>
> (1539–44)

Human willpower can subjugate the impersonal force of chance just as shuffling, usually a randomizing act, here ensures that Selimus will get the card, or the royal status, he wants; and with no supreme being, there is no absolute morality to call it cheating. In turn, those who fail to take the initiative and accept their lowly station in life are not principled but contemptibly pusillanimous: as Richard says, 'Conscience is but a word that cowards use' (5. 6. 39). These characters free themselves by, as it were, emptying out the universe of its obstructions and inhibitions, and in so doing make themselves the most charismatic figures in their respective plays: it is always more fun to bustle than to jostle, and more theatrically exciting to watch, too.

The problem is that, in the end, jostle we must. In *Hamlet*, the rebels who seek to elect Laertes King of Denmark are said to be acting as if 'the world were now but to begin' (4. 5. 101); but in fact the world is far from new and far from flexible. Tamburlaine may have been exciting as the maker of his own identity and future, but the equivocal nature of his status as a cult figure is clear in an incident that took place in 1593, six years after his first appearance. That spring, a xenophobic poem threatening a massacre of the resident Fleming population was found, to official consternation, posted on the wall of the Dutch church in London; its author had signed himself 'Tamburlaine'. The association of Marlowe's hero with the seizure and exercise of power made his name a liberating mouthpiece for secret antipathies that were frowned upon by society's masters, and which could not be expressed in one's own person without the risk of state reprisals. But that pseudonymous circumspection is also to the point: if the poet identified himself with Tamburlaine, he is nevertheless least like him in assuming his name, because in doing so he pulls back from committing himself. The appeal of the character ultimately had little application to the constraining complexities of reality: he may easily be able to dominate the play's open landscape of atlas-derived place-names, but closer to home the will to power is held in check by the desire to continue living a safe, quiet life.

We can see this in another recurrent feature of 1590s history plays concerned with social mobility: their treatment of popular rebellions like the Jack Cade revolt in *Henry VI, Part 2*. At one level they draw overtly on the fantasy appeal of *Tamburlaine* in the way insurgents seek to appropriate the opulence and status of high rank, imaged in a familiar lush style: in *Edward IV, Part 1* (anonymous, but sometimes attributed to Heywood, 1599), the aristocratic traitor Falconbridge promises his plebeian followers,

> We will be masters of the Mint ourselves,
> And set our own stamp on the golden coin.
> We'll shoe our neighing coursers with no worse
> Than the purest silver that is sold in Cheap [Cheapside].
> At Leadenhall we'll sell pearls by the peck

As now the mealmen use to sell their meal.
In Westminster we'll keep a solemn court,
And build it bigger to receive our men.

(A5ʳ)

Yet if this is attractive, there is another side to rebellion. Elizabethan stage mobs are typically portrayed as capable of atrocities such as killing people for their literacy, as in *Henry VI, Part 2*, or even, in *Julius Caesar* (1599), for being a bad poet. Tamburlaine's majestic ambition was to 'ride in triumph through Persepolis' (2. 5. 50); if there is something slightly mock-heroic about Falconbridge's corresponding wish to 'ride in triumph thorough Cheap to Paul's' (C4ᵛ), there is something terrifying about it too.

Tamburlaine's real-life application was limited in metaphysical as well as in social and political terms: the culture's dominant assumptions about the universe included the notion of an all-powerful and just God, so the play's determinedly materialist version of history could be considered a somewhat partial representation of reality. Such an objection would, of course, best be satisifed by the received theory of tragedy which Marlowe had overturned—that is, by the kind of play in which the hubristic hero misplaces his faith in material things and is finally laid low by the implacable force of destiny, or Fortune, or the gods. It is understandable that some later writers should have reopened this as an available mode of interpretation, particularly when materialism had escalated into the even more provocative creed of atheism. Richard III, for example, is defeated at Bosworth by an enemy who prays before the battle and afterwards attributes the victory to providence. Today we tend to feel embarrassed by this kind of overt Christianity in Shakespeare's tragedies, which can look like an unworthily naïve retreat into conventional pieties, whereas in its own time it was probably just the concluding imposition of a relatively uncontentious world-view; yet our modern unease is not entirely anachronistic. The play may resemble the old tragedy in trumping Richard's libertarian atheism with a higher dimension of existence; the difference is that in this ending the play gainsays one of its own most fundamental pleasures, the amoral exuberance of its central character. It may reflect the inescapability of the real world, like the Dutch Church writer's pragmatic decision not to put his own name to his poison-pen poem, but, as in *Doctor Faustus*, it is not a conclusion to which we can wholeheartedly assent.

Tragedy and Humanism

Tragedies always end in disappointment: that is what makes them tragic. The *Tamburlaine* plays were appealing, and refreshing, because they focused the sixteenth century's new philosophical sense of the boundless potential of humanity: Marlowe's hero creates himself and his destiny in the face of all social and political opposition. Tragedy proper attends to the obverse, the hero's failure to realize his full human potential, either because of the kind of world he lives in or the kind of self he makes through his own actions. As such, it too rests on the humanistic view of man which found its most eloquent spokesman in Hamlet: 'What a piece of work is a man! How noble in reason, how infinite in faculty, in form and moving how express and admirable, in action how like an angel, in apprehension how like a god—the beauty of the world, the paragon of animals!' (2. 2. 305–9) Alone among Shakespeare's tragic heroes, the Prince of Denmark has himself a developed sense of the tragic, which here activates the same disappointment, even before he continues, 'to me what is this quintessence of dust?' (309–10). We can see his mind's eye turning downward when he says that man, who bears comparison with angels and with gods, is also the paragon of animals, for that is humanism's dangerous trapdoor. The period's orthodoxy, inherited from medieval Christianity, gave mankind a comfortingly fixed place in the cosmic hierarchy between angels and beasts, but the humanist thinkers, whose protean creation myth Hamlet echoes, offered the more glorious and more frightening prospect of self-definition: man could rise to the perfection of divinity, but only with the corollary that he might alternatively degenerate to the ranks of the beasts; to use Hamlet's own terms, he could be Hyperion or a satyr. It is the same vertical scale that runs between *Tamburlaine* and tragedy, and the meaning of either depends on the contrasting possibility of the other: whereas, in the older conception of the genre, the mere fact of going down to destruction was tragic in itself, in *Doctor Faustus* damnation is tragic because there is also salvation. The essence of the experience is our sense of shortfall, of the disparity between the central character's potential and his achievement.

This is one reason why the tragedies of the period often focus on heroic characters. Many are war heroes like Tamburlaine: Titus Andronicus, Macbeth, and Coriolanus all return home early in their respective plays having taken a decisive part in winning a military victory, and Othello too has a formidable battlefield reputation. Others have a comparable superiority of imaginative or intellectual capacity, like Hamlet or, arguably, Brutus. Before Kyd and Marlowe, the greatness of office alone was enough to define a tragic hero, because all he had to do was fall from that high estate; but in the new tragedy, the heroes have a greatness of inherent character which defines their human potential and so marks out the extent of the tragic loss and waste which their fall entails. 'O thou Othello, that was once so good' (5. 2. 297): the sense of the superlative and the past tense in which it is mentioned are both to the point.

The tragedies which are usually felt to be easiest to analyse in this respect are the ones which have an early focus on a single, momentous act of will, like Lear's giving away his kingdom, or Faustus' signing away his soul, which creates the circumstances that lead on to destruction. This is a development of Aristotle's analysis of tragedy as proceeding from an act of significant error which he called *hamartia*. In the old tragedy, this might be a hubristic act which calls down the punishment of the gods; Tamburlaine's burning the Koran alludes to this concept in order to undermine it. In the new, however, it is a deed which fundamentally reduces a character's future options, delivering a previously free agent into the bondage of circumstance: there is an emphasis first on the process of choosing—to kill, to conspire, to conjure, to be or not to be—which is dramatized in the hero's soliloquies, and then on the consequences of that choice. Tragedies of crime are especially clear-cut in this respect, because the *hamartia*, usually murder, is both a moral rubicon and an event which overtly requires further action to deceive or frustrate the public mechanisms of justice. Thomas Middleton puts it well in *The Changeling* (1622) when Beatrice–Joanna, who has procured the death of her fiancé, is told that she has become 'the deed's creature' (3. 4. 136): it has remade her, and sin must now pluck on sin if she is not to be exposed as a murderess. Similarly, Macbeth is deluding himself when he says, after the assassination of Banquo, 'I am in blood | Stepped in so far that, should I wade no more, | Returning were as tedious as go o'er.' (3. 4. 135–7) He is not free to turn back, because his murders cannot be undone: it is symbolically apt that his wife, in her sleepwalking state, should believe herself unable to wash the blood off her hands.

However, there are many other tragedies in which the hero's free will is severely curtailed from the first. Beaumont and Fletcher's *The Maid's Tragedy* (1611) also begins with an act of choice which cannot be reversed, though not one that appears obviously tragic in its implications: the young courtier Amintor gets married. As the action develops, however, it becomes clear that the freedom of that choice was nugatory, because it was taken in ignorance: what Amintor didn't know was that his bride is also the King's mistress and is under orders not to consummate the marriage. In this kind of tragedy there is a sense not so much of the greatness as the pathetic littleness of the characters, and their suffering is a consequence not of choice but of compulsion. Occasionally, as in *The Spanish Tragedy*, it arises from the implacable and inscrutable operations of a metaphysical dimension of reality which is indifferent to individual human pain. In *Romeo and Juliet*, for example, the lovers' bad luck is so systematic, ranging from the accident of their birth as members of rival families to the miscarriage of Friar Laurence's letter to Romeo, that it is hard not to agree with the Friar in seeing the purposeful opposition of fate: 'A greater power than we can contradict | Hath thwarted our intents' (5. 3. 153–4). More often, however, the malevolent greater power is that of the state and its grandees, who use and destroy people whenever doing so is expedient to cement their authority, as the King dupes Amintor into being a respectable front for his lechery, and as the agents of the Roman state cause oppositional voices to 'disappear' in Ben Jonson's *Sejanus' Fall* (1603).

Both types of tragedy evoke regret, but of different kinds: one is regret for the annihilation of a human being, the other for the bleak and circumscribing condition of humanity. One owes much to Marlowe and the other to Kyd, but they both rest on the disappointed hope for something better which *Tamburlaine* had fostered. When King Lear meets the naked Edgar in the guise of Tom o' Bedlam, he asks the fundamental question which all tragic events pose: 'Is man no more than this?' (3. 4. 96–7). His answer is a nihilistic negative: no dignity, no expectations, no hope. Ours will be more equivocal: whatever calamity strikes, whatever tyranny galls, however petty or wretched the hero finally becomes, man can be more. That is what tragedy means.

3

Comedy's Metamorphosis

Tradition has it that Ben Jonson's first major comedy, *Every Man in His Humour*, was nearly rejected when he offered it to the Lord Chamberlain's Men in 1598: it was given a cursory reading and was on the point of being sent back when Shakespeare happened to look it over, recognized its merits, and intervened on its behalf. We don't know whether this ever actually happened (there are reasons to think it did not), but the story contains nevertheless a symbolic truth about the events of the late 1590s. It was first told by Shakespeare's biographer Nicholas Rowe in 1709, in order to show the playwright's personal generosity in giving a break to the man who was to become his principal competitor and his shrewdest critic; but it also reflects, distorted in the passage of eleven decades, the changing circumstances of the play-writing profession at this point in his career. During the 1590s, Shakespeare became the London theatre's pre-eminent dramatist not only through talent but also by default. During the middle years of the decade, virtually every other experienced playwright disappeared from the scene: Robert Greene ate himself to death in 1592, Marlowe was murdered in 1593, Kyd died a pauper in 1594, and Peele succumbed to venereal disease in 1596; Lyly lived on for ten more years, writing begging letters to prominent courtiers, but he had never successfully transferred his work to the adult stage when his boy company closed down in 1590. For a while, Shakespeare had no serious rivals: new writers were not entering the profession to fill the dead men's shoes, perhaps because the London theatre business was at its least stable in the years 1593–5, when plague and playhouse closures bankrupted several companies. It was with the return of better times in the later part of the decade that fresh talent emerged: not only Jonson but Thomas Dekker, John Marston, and, most important of all, George Chapman.

Rowe also meant to illustrate Shakespeare's superior eye for aesthetic quality, but the legend equally shows his commercial astuteness, and not only in the ability to pick a winner. In the story, the theatre functionaries who are on the point of rejecting *Every Man in His Humour* are going to tell Jonson that the play is of no use to the company. Unless they were just being obtuse, this might indicate more than the wording of a standard rejection. Jonson's play must indeed have seemed very unlike the sort of thing the Lord Chamberlain's Men usually presented, if we can take Shakespeare's comedies as typical (as we must, for no other Lord Chamberlain's comedies survive from this period). They always tell a clear, romantic story, usually defined by a narrative source, whereas Jonson's sourceless and socially realistic play rambles through a sequence of comic incidents driven by the varying combinations of characters on stage. Conversely, Jonson's action is tightly contained within a single April day, whereas, with the notable exceptions of *The Comedy of Errors* (*c.*1592) and *The Tempest* (1611), Shakespeare tends to let events sprawl with little indication of the precise timescale. In all these respects, *Every Man in His Humour* was not in the company's established comic mode; but it was also very similar to the new kind of comedies being presented at the Rose playhouse on the other side of the Thames by London's other acting company, the Admiral's Men. Jonson had, in fact, been working for them as a scriptwriter for about a year; now he was offering a play in their 'house style' to their principal competitors.

So Rowe's story is also about the difference between small men, with their narrow sense of company identity, and the expansive imagination of a great man, who can fashion that identity anew as circumstances dictate. That is why it probably isn't literally true: the story requires the script readers to have been extraordinarily imperceptive or ill-briefed, which is unlikely, and *Every Man in His Humour* to have been extraordinarily revolutionary, which it wasn't. The revolution had already happened, and, as we shall see, Shakespeare was already in the process of refashioning the company's output in its wake. In any event, Jonson's play was produced by the Lord Chamberlain's Men, with Shakespeare in the cast; it was successful enough to remain in their repertory for more than thirty years.

New Fashions and an Old Genre

In the summer of 1597, English drama killed its father—which is, at least metaphorically, how all true progress begins. We can see how suddenly it happened if we look at the different ways Shakespeare chooses to spoof stage rhetoric in two closely associated plays. When Sir John Oldcastle (who was to become Falstaff) impersonates the King in *Henry IV, Part 1* (early 1597), he says he will perform the role 'in King Cambyses' vein' (2. 5. 390). The allusion is to the most commercially successful of all early Elizabethan plays, Thomas Preston's *Cambyses, King of Persia* (1561), and when Sir John begins his part it is indeed an effective parody of that period's dramatic speech, with its pedantic adjectives and unintentionally silly metaphors: 'For God's sake, lords, convey my tristful Queen, | For tears do stop the floodgates of her eyes.' (2. 5. 397–8) Nine months or so later, in *Henry IV, Part 2* (1597–8), Shakespeare chose a very much closer target:

> Shall pack-horses
> And hollow pampered jades of Asia,
> Which cannot go but thirty mile a day,
> Compare with Caesars and with cannibals,
> And Trojan Greeks?
> Nay, rather damn them with King Cerberus,
> And let the welkin roar.
>
> (2. 4. 160–6)

With its high vocabulary, classical particularity, and powerful pentameters, this is supposed to sound like Marlowe, complete with a direct lift from the best-remembered scene in *The Second Part of Tamburlaine*. Ensign Pistol, who speaks the lines, was only the first of a run of comic braggarts who filch their eloquence from the drama of the recent past. Of course, Pistol is ignorant as well as bombastic—Cerberus was not a king, the Greeks could never be Trojan, and when he says 'cannibals' he is probably misremembering the Carthaginian general Hannibal—but it was not only in such a mouth that Marlowe's barnstorming tragic rhetoric now sounded ridiculous. At around the same time that Shakespeare created Pistol, the satirist Joseph Hall wrote mockingly of the stage's 'huff-cap terms and thundering threats':

ten years after it was new, a style that had once been excitingly majestic now seemed outmoded and overwrought.[1] Theatrical taste was on the turn.

Marlowe himself was already dead—both Jonson in *Every Man in His Humour* and Shakespeare in *As You Like It* (1600) pointedly mention the fact when they quote from his non-dramatic poetry— and now his mode of heroic tragedy was dying too. It may not be relevant, but it is certainly apt, that 1597 should have been the year in which Edward Alleyn, the thirty-year-old star most associated with Marlowe's leading roles, gave up acting. That summer, between the writing of one part of *Henry IV* and the other, drama became self-consciously modern in a way that was later epitomized in Jonson's prologue to *Every Man in His Humour*. He rejects the stage's established subject matter, notably including Shakespeare's civil war plays of *Henry VI*, as contemptuously as Marlowe did the 'rhyming mother wits' of the early 1580s in his prologue to *Tamburlaine the Great*; he also dismisses the kind of characters created by Marlowe and Alleyn, calling them 'monsters', grotesque travesties of human beings. It seems to have been a temporary phase, which was drawing to an end in 1601 when the Admiral's Men decided to revive *The Spanish Tragedy* as part of a themed 'Spanish' season. What is significant is that they also decided not to use Kyd's original script, and hired Jonson to produce an adaptation; *Doctor Faustus* got similar treatment when it returned to the stage the following year. Though once again bankable, these old classics still needed to be refashioned to take account of new tastes and new sensibilities, or, in Jonson's terms, to turn their 'monsters' into men.

Fundamentally, the change was a reversal of genre fashion. This is the import of Jonson's prologue assertion of *Every Man in His Humour*'s verisimilitude: the play contains

> deeds and language such as men do use,
> And persons such as Comedy would choose
> When she would show an image of the times,
> And sport with human follies, not with crimes.

Dramatic speech turned from the high style to the low: there is more prose in the plays of this period, along with an increasingly flexible use of verse, without the magnificent metrical regularity and end-stopping that characterized Marlowe's writing. Plotting and characterization underwent a corresponding change of focus: late 1590s plays tend to deal more with the private than with the political, and tend to emphasize the pettiness of humanity rather than its expansive greatness and potential. For a decade after *Tamburlaine*, it had been tragedy that most excited and inspired London audiences; but in 1597, taste comprehensively turned towards comedy.

It was inevitable that dramatic fashion should eventually move in this direction when it moved away from the Marlovian heroic style, because comedy was the genre which had been least affected by the *Tamburlaine* revolution of 1587. Of course, Marlowe's stylistic innovations were irresistible, but comedy was not responsive to his thematic concerns at any more than a superficial level. *Tamburlaine the Great* is in a sense a tragedy with a comic ending, in that the hero gets married instead of dying as anticipated, but, as discussed in the last chapter, it is also an ending which radically and fundamentally changes the order of things. Comedy, in contrast, ends by re-establishing a fitly ordered society as it was then conceived: lovers are married, families reunited, and shrews tamed, and any disharmonious elements are purged away. A few comedies capitalized on the fashionable interest in social hierarchy which Marlowe initiated, but ultimately the comic structure limits and contains the disruptive energies of the aspirant imagination.

We can see this process at its clearest in the most unlikely of all Tamburlaine's many inheritors: Christopher Sly, the drunken beggar in *The Taming of the Shrew* (*c.*1591) who is deluded into thinking himself a lord. The dream of ascent from the lowest to the highest strata of society is expressed with the usual potent sensuality:

> Carry him gently to my fairest chamber
> And hang it round with all my wanton pictures.
> Balm his foul head in warm distillèd waters,
> And burn sweet wood to make the lodging sweet.

> (Ind. 1. 44–7)

But there is an obvious and important difference: whereas Tamburlaine achieves greatness through force of arms and force of personality, Christopher Sly has it thrust upon him; it is all a practical joke, and the joke is on him. The funniest moment of the sequence is his realization, 'Upon my life, I am a lord indeed' (Ind. 2. 71), precisely because he is not and never could be: authority and control remain with the real lord playing the prank, a point reinforced in the alternative, non-Shakespearian version of the play which ends with Sly being unceremoniously returned to the alehouse whence he came. The emphasis on the physical luxury into which he is transported may follow *Tamburlaine* in making ambition seem attractive, but in this genre a man never has any real prospect of permanent advancement: in the main action of *The Taming of the Shrew*, the master Lucentio swaps clothes and identities with his servant Tranio, but they change back before the end; those who want to stay above their station, like the would-be 'Count' Malvolio in *Twelfth Night* (1601), usually end up having their subordinate status forcefully reasserted.

The Comedy of Love

Before 1597, then, comedy had developed only gently, unruffled by the radical changes in the rest of English drama. In the 1580s, the genre was dominated by the brittle, witty plays of Lyly, and in the 1590s by Shakespeare. There are some obvious differences between the two dramatists' work, but also an underlying similarity of technique and tone. Lyly wrote for boy actors, a medium whose avowed artifice is reflected in the complex rhetorical figures of his writing, quite unlike the freer-flowing dialogue Shakespeare gives his less diminutive performers. However, both create comic situations through the artful orchestration of confusion and misunderstanding; and though Lyly usually draws his themes from classical mythology and Shakespeare from modern Italian models, both deal with the pains and triumphs that arise in the pursuit of worldly love and happiness.

In *Every Man out of His Humour* (1599), Jonson's follow-up to *Every Man in*, there is a sardonic description of a typical romantic comedy plot: 'a duke to be in love with a countess, and that countess to be in love with the duke's son, and the son to love the lady's waiting-maid: some such cross-wooing, with a clown to their servingman' (3. 6. 196–9). It is a familiar scenario: many comedies of the 1580s and early 1590s feature groups of heterosexual lovers who do not fall neatly into even pairs. In Lyly's *Sappho and Phao* (1583), for example, Venus makes Phao both overpoweringly attractive to women and uninterested in them, and most of the problems of Shakespeare's *The Two Gentlemen of Verona* (*c.*1593) arise because the title characters both love the same woman, leaving Proteus' former girlfriend Julia on the shelf. Such things can happen because love is portrayed as a random, capricious force, often personified by Lyly as a mischievous Cupid wantonly tormenting human beings with his arrows of desire. In Shakespeare, its origins are generally more mysterious, as they are in life: the only equivalent to Cupid in any of his comedies is Puck, the bungling sprite in *A Midsummer Night's Dream* (1595) who puts the love-juice on the wrong boy's eyes to produce another 'cross-wooing' and then enjoys the resultant complications; but unlike Cupid he has simply made a mistake in carrying out his master's more benevolent plan to square the play's love triangle. The triangle itself already existed at the beginning, one of the messy circumstances of reality to be changed into order and harmony through the working of the comic action. Whatever its origins, though, love's effects are usually the same: it makes characters do unreasonable things and pursue apparently unsuitable or unresponsive partners, and one of the pleasures of comedy is to watch their antics and to say, with Puck, 'Lord, what fools these mortals be' (3. 2. 115).

It is a pleasure necessarily founded on the expectation and eventual achievement of a happy ending. Romantic comedies usually move towards a conclusion involving the successful union of one or more young couples: 'the catastrophe is a nuptial' (4. 1. 76), as Don Armado pretentiously puts it in *Love's Labours Lost* (1595; *catastrophe* was the technical term for a play's dénouement, not necessarily a tragic one). Without an underlying confidence that events will work out for the best, Jonson's story of 'cross-wooing' would begin to look like Sartre's portrayal of hell in *Huis Clos* (1944) as an eternity of unrequited love. In this respect it is not an overstatement to call Cupid's activities a torment: the conjunction between the power of the emotion and the force of the opposition means that love's process in comedy is often a painful one. That pain is only bearable, and a detached response like Puck's possible, through the knowledge that the play is not a tragedy, though it may contain the potential to be one; that, this time, power and circumstance will prove tractable, and love will conquer all.

If we judge the action solely in terms of the outcome towards which it moves, though, we risk underestimating the obstacles and dangers which the lovers must overcome in order to get there. Sometimes the problem may be the recalcitrance of the desired partner, who needs to be brought to a maturer understanding of love and its transcendent importance, like the two-timing Proteus in *The Two Gentlemen of Verona* or the haughty nymphs in Lyly's *Love's Metamorphosis* (1590). But there may also be external impediments: the couple may be kept apart by a disparity in their rank, as in *Fair Em, the Miller's Daughter of Manchester* (anonymous, 1590), or an obstructive father like Egeus in *A Midsummer Night's Dream*, whose preferred son-in-law is not the suitor Hermia loves; they may also have to face an unsympathetic public authority, like the Athenian law which presents Hermia with the stark alternatives of loveless marriage, death, or lifelong chastity. These are not trivial matters, even when the state is not directly involved. For example, it is easy, but mistaken, to think of comic fathers just as silly, interfering old men who don't ultimately get their way. In Lyly's *Mother Bombie* (1590), the lovers Candius and Livia are in danger of being married off to a pair of wealthy imbeciles, a situation which causes Candius to inveigh against their fathers with an indignant adolescent nostalgia for the nurturing parent of childhood:

Parents in these days are grown peevish: they rock their children in their cradles till they sleep, and cross them about their bridals till their hearts ache. Marriage among them is become a market. 'What will you give with your daughter?' 'What jointure will you make for your son?' And many a match is broken off for a penny more or less, as though they could not afford their children at such a price; when none should cheapen such ware but affection, and none buy it but love.   (1. 3. 90–7)

Beneath the artfully turned phrases there is anger and anguish, generated by a real collision of mighty opposites. There are strong power relations involved: the Duke in *A Midsummer Night's Dream* may be overstating things when he tells Hermia, 'To you your father should be as a god' (1. 1. 47), but in Tudor political theory a father's authority over his children was considered a little simulacrum of a king's over his subjects. Economic reality is also a factor: Lyly's two fathers, though clearly misguided, are shown to be pragmatic and conscientious in their attention to the financial basis for their children's marriage. The idealistic love of Candius and Livia is sympathetic, but obviously impractical: almost every circumstance is against them.

Comic plots usually happen because lovers refuse to be practical: the emotional force of love is strong enough to rupture the bonds of their unwelcome circumstances. One way in which they liberate themselves is through disguise: that is how Candius and Livia are eventually able to marry under their fathers' noses. A new identity, albeit a temporary one, can allow a character to overleap the conventions and social relations that confine their usual selves: Lacy, the aristocratic lover in Greene's *Friar Bacon and Friar Bungay* (1589), crosses the striations of social hierarchy to woo his plebeian sweetheart in the guise of a Suffolk farmer; and in *The Two Gentlemen of Verona*, Julia transcends her gender to follow Proteus to Milan, a journey more hazardous for an unaccompanied woman than for a page. In every case, the characters seek to bypass an obstruction by displacing themselves, a metaphor which Shakespeare makes literal in *A Midsummer Night's Dream*. Here the lovers take the most drastic step of all, and drop out altogether: when Hermia and her boyfriend abscond from Athens and travel into the wood, they comprehensively reject the restrictions and limitations of civilization, with its unjust laws and antagonistic structures of authority; but in doing so, they also forgo its protection.

A Midsummer Night's Dream contains not only a potential but an actual tragedy. Fortunately it is the unintentionally amusing one performed by Bottom and his friends at the end of the play, but beyond its inherent opportunities for laughter it also works to emphasize the lovers' narrow escape in the main action. Its story of Pyramus and Thisbe deals with two young people whose love is opposed by their parents, and who leave the city for an assignation, encounter a lion, and, through a pair of tragic misunderstandings, both end up dead. The parallel with Hermia's own story scarcely needs pointing out— except that she and her friends meet nothing more threatening than Puck, and come back alive. In this they are fortunate, for the wood is shown to be a dangerous place full of savage and poisonous fauna. At one point the waking Hermia speaks of being attacked by a snake, and it takes a moment for her, and perhaps also the audience, to realize that she was dreaming: we have already seen the fairies use incantations to keep the spiders and snakes away from the sleeping Titania, a defence not shared by the intruding mortals. Their 'cross-wooing' is resolved in the forest by the application of love-juice, but it could have been by death.

It is worth stressing the possibility of physical harm because displacement is never envisaged as a permanent solution. An obvious illustration is Lyly's *Love's Metamorphosis*, in which Cupid helps out three amorous shepherds by temporarily changing their disdainful nymphs into, respectively, animal, vegetable, and mineral forms. This would be a pointless exercise if the nymphs were to remain metamorphosed forever: the intention is to discipline them into recognizing that, as beautiful women, they should submit to love. In comedy the ultimate objective of the itinerant or transformed lovers is always to return home safely, to revert to their own forms and identities, with love triumphant over circumstances. The risk is that their initial action may have consequences, such as a fatal encounter with a poisonous snake or a hungry lion, which make that impossible: Cupid's metamorphosis does not teach the nymphs the lesson intended, only encourages them to ask, not unreasonably, why they should love men who have had them turned into stones and the like; while in *Friar Bacon and Friar Bungay*, Lacy is suspected of treason when the King hears that he has been gallivanting around the country dressed in rustic clothes. The course of true love never runs smooth because it is the rough patches which create the comic plot—and the rougher they are, the more they enhance the joyousness of the eventual happy ending.

If audiences respond to comedy on two levels, with both an amused, Puck-like observation of confusion and a humane engagement with the lovers' trials and aspirations, then comic endings are correspondingly multivalent. In part, it is a process of restoration: the characters' displacement creates a complicated knot of error, disorder, and delusion which is finally unravelled when they regain their true identities. In the course of the action noblemen may have become commoners and vice versa, and women may have assumed the roles and status of men, but in the end these displacements and disruptions are undone: disguises are removed and ranks reaffirmed, and everyone returns to their proper place, unjustly banished lords to the court and confidence tricksters to the underworld. Yet on a different level these endings also achieve more: there is a net gain. In *Fair Em*, the miller's daughter is eventually able to marry one of her aristocratic suitors, not through some pleasing change in the over-rigid social structure that has kept them apart, but because she and her father turn out themselves to be members of the nobility. In returning to the court, they transcend not only their disguise but also the political disgrace that originally drove them into hiding, and the play's ultimate harmony lies not only in the consummation of a love affair in marriage but in the healing of a larger breach in the commonwealth. At a pettier domestic level, too, parents must eventually accept their children's choice of marriage partner, however grudgingly: 'these things cannot be recalled,' says Candius' father in *Mother Bombie*, 'therefore as good consent' (5. 3. 243–4). This goes beyond the victory of true love over fatherly error: it is also the happy reconciliation of a once broken family.

As well as a 'cross-wooing', Jonson's formula for romantic comedy also specifies a clown as the servingman. This is one of the principal differences between Shakespearian and Lylian comedy: Shakespeare usually features a clown and Lyly does not, because the adult compan-ies usually employed a principal low-comedy actor (not, of course, a circus clown) to take care of the verbal and visual slapstick, whereas there was no comparable figure among the boys for whom Lyly wrote. The character type derives from the witty slaves of Roman comedy, generally updated into an exasperating servant of one of the principals, like Grumio in *The Taming of the Shrew*. The servant–master relation-ship is in part that of comic and straight man, as in the scene where Grumio finds it hard to understand that, in commanding 'knock me here soundly' (1. 2. 8), Petruccio is not asking for a beating but means him to knock on the door. The clown has an anarchic vigour which mocks the pretensions of his betters, whether it be Petruccio's slightly arcane grammar or, in *Friar Bacon and Friar Bungay*, dramatic speech's comprehensive shift into blank verse, which the comic servant Miles defies in one scene by insistently speaking in old-fashioned rhyming Skeltonics 'And yet, Master Doctor, to speak like a proctor, | And tell unto you what is veriment and true.' (7. 61–2) In this respect such roles could do more for a play than just elicit belly-laughs.

In *Fair Em*, there is a scene in which the miller's servant, Trotter, attempts to kiss the heroine and bustle her off to church for a quick wedding. Em's response is to point out that her father is his master, and the episode is aborted by the arrival of her first high-born suitor, who has already been agonizing about the impediments of rank: 'A miller's daughter, says the multitude, | Should not be lovèd of a gentleman.' (4.8–9) Trotter's actions contradict, from the opposite direction, this principle of loving within one's own class: for him the movement from desire to consummation is simple and direct, unhindered by the demands and conventions of civilized society save for the barest form of contract, a 'mumbled-up' marriage. In effect, he ignores the social structures which the play takes as a given, and in his earthy sexuality he stands counter to the dominant romantic tone. There is an animal realism to him (even his name has comically porcine associations) which Shakespeare later developed and emphasized in *The Two Gentlemen of Verona*'s Lance, who not only takes the blame for his dog's urinating (or defecating?) under the table but actually says he did it himself, and in Bottom, who literally becomes, at least from the neck up, an animal well-known for its large genitalia, an ass.

It is relevant that it should be Bottom and his colleagues who later provide the inset play which focuses the action's tragic potential. The clown is often the alternative, contrapuntal voice who stands for the other side of life which comedy excludes. He tends to be characterized by blockish stupidity rather than wit, to be interested in sex rather than love, to be a figure of realism rather than romance. In all these respects, he was in danger of becoming obsolete when comic fashion changed in the second half of the 1590s.

The Comedy of Humours

The new comedy was more character-centred, more socially realistic, and more concerned with the vagaries of human sexuality. The change was driven by the success of a single play that was to be as influential for comedy as *Tamburlaine* had been for tragedy. 'We have here a new play of humours in very great request,' wrote John Chamberlain to an out-of-town friend that summer, 'and I was drawn along to it by the common applause'. This was *The Comedy of Humours* (now usually called by its published title, *A Humorous Day's Mirth*), written by the outstanding comic talent of the new intake of dramatists, George Chapman. It was first performed by the Admiral's Men at the Rose in May 1597, and was quite unlike anything which had been seen before: there is no real plot, only a sequence of comic intrigues orchestrated by a courtly prankster, Lemot, in which the young gallants plot to frustrate the quirks and jealousies of the older characters. The attentive eye may detect traces of *The Two Gentlemen of Verona* and *Love's Labours Lost*, but as a whole it is a smart, self-consciously new and modern piece of writing based on the underlying premise that people are in themselves funny enough to sustain a comic action, without the need for a conventional story: the central appeal lies in human behaviour rather than in the working-out of events. Chamberlain was disappointed, perhaps finding it too insubstantial a confection: 'my opinion of it is (as the fellow said of the shearing of hogs) that there was a great cry for so little wool.'[2] It seems to have been a minority opinion, though: the financial records of the theatre's owner, Philip Henslowe, show what a commercial triumph *The Comedy of Humours* was, bringing in takings comparable with those for Marlowe's plays in their heyday.

The play was the first English comedy to have a realistic modern setting. Since that setting happens to be Paris, this fact is easily overlooked in favour of a range of plays which soon followed and whose action takes place on the hither side of the English channel in Windsor, Oxfordshire, and the city of London. But its novelty, of course, lay in contrast with what had gone before. Lyly had nominally set a couple of his plays in England, but in *Gallathea* (1584) it is an England where the goddess Venus frolics with her nymphs and maidens are annually sacrificed to a sea monster, and even in the less magical environment of *Mother Bombie* the characters are 'Englishmen' with names like Memphio and Dromio: England is just the diaphanous fancy dress of Lyly's usual classical landscape. Shakespeare's romantic comedies, too, are firmly Mediterranean or arboreal in their settings, their overt focus resolutely elsewhere. *The Comedy of Humours*, however, begins in a private garden and gravitates towards a city ordinary, or eating-house, where most of the intrigues are played out.

Verone's ordinary can be seen as a place of retreat and refreshment for the courtly characters, as Shakespeare later made the pastoral world when he returned to romantic comedy in *As You Like It*. The difference is that this is not only its dramatic but its man-made function: with its napkins and tablecloths and candlesticks, all physically present on stage rather than just represented in descriptive speeches like the landscape of Arden, it is an environment created for the purpose of giving noblemen and others somewhere to eat and drink, gamble and enjoy themselves. Shakespeare's woodlands are places where the characters temporarily give up control of their lives, where it is chance or fairies that make the running; but a corollary of Chapman's this-worldly setting is that events never slip significantly beyond human management, and are directed by those best able to master the environment. The start of the play both emphasizes this and mocks the expectation of supernatural intervention: in the opening scene, a jealous and impotent Count leaves an unsigned message for his religious wife in her locked garden, expecting her to infer that it was left by God rather than by someone with an extra set of keys. A lottery at the end makes a similar point: presided over by a maidservant dressed up as Fortune, it nevertheless delivers wittily accurate judgements on all who participate; what seemed to be a game of chance turns out to have been fixed by Lemot. This degree of human control means that, unlike in most romantic comedies, there is little real danger: provided that one can accept the central device of repeatedly playing practical jokes on people, there is a refreshing absence of malice which makes the conclusion—in which the King invites all the characters to a feast at court—not a restoration of order or a healing of wounds but simply a reassertion of the prevailing tone of geniality.

The joker Lemot is the focus of the audience's engagement with the action, partly because he creates most of it, but partly too because this process depends on his superior sense of the other characters' limitations. It is typical that one of his games should involve guessing in advance what people will say when he engages them in conversation, because in a larger sense predictability is the essence of the sport: he prods people and watches them jump, manipulates them in such a way as to expose their inherent idiosyncrasies of personality, or 'humours' as the Elizabethans called them. The joke is that the characters will always behave as expected, and the pleasure of the comedy lies in the interplay of their dominant character traits: this is the fundamental originality of conception memorialized in the title.

The idea of a plotless comedy written entirely around 'humours' probably arose out of Chapman's previous play for the company, *The Blind Beggar of Alexandria* (1596). Though sometimes treated as a comedy, it is really a romance with comic interludes, set in a landscape of near-eastern potentates and exotic geographical references. In this it is one of the last plays to exploit *Tamburlaine's* success before fashion and taste turned elsewhere. The title character, like Tamburlaine, was born a shepherd, and he has the usual dynastic ambitions, though not the single-mindedness: 'For till the time that I may claim the crown, | I mean to spend my time in sports of love.' (1. 123–4) It is through the comic devices of disguise and mistaken identity that he does both. The play can be seen as a clever reversal of *The Comedy of Errors*: instead of two men temporarily conflated into the identity of one, Chapman presents a single character leading a quadruple life as beggar and usurer, mad lover and heroic soldier. The action presents him juggling these different personas, and finally dismantling the three of lowest rank so that the beggar becomes a king.

Chapman effectively invented 'humours' characterization as a response to the dynamics of this scenario. In *The Comedy of Errors*, the Antipholus twins are carefully differentiated characters who happen to look identical; they behave towards other people in quite distinct ways, but to those people they are who they look like, not how they act. In *The Blind Beggar*, in contrast, behaviour and appearance work together in each of the title character's roles to create the impression of a distinct individual. This is not just because the different identities are calculated deceptions rather than happenstance as in Shakespeare's play. The coherence of a dramatic character derives in part from continuity: his appearance and behaviour remain similar from scene to scene. When that character is adopted as a disguise or second identity, there is a further requirement: he must not only be continuous with himself but also distinct from the other persona, and this is multiplied exponentially with each new role. Chapman's beggar has split himself into four different identities, and for the deception to succeed each of them must look and act quite differently from each of the others; or, to put it another way, each character must always be unmistakably himself. The effect is to limit the amount of variation available within the primary need for coherence: each of his roles is consistently the same, rather than just similar. As the mad lover, for example, he always wears the same velvet coat, and, since most people change their clothes from time to time, this continuity of appearance is also a behavioural eccentricity that makes him even more individually distinctive. In effect, each of the roles is defined by a 'humour'.

The Blind Beggar was the Rose's most profitable play of 1596, but it was probably not the implausible romance plot which won it such an enthusiastic reception: when it was published two years later, it came to the printer in a version heavily cut in favour of the comic material. This centred not only on quirky characters but on sexual intrigues: the title character's multiple-identity 'sports of love' involve a deliberately bigamous marriage, after which he schemes to sleep with each wife in the persona of the other's husband. Before this, explicit treatments of adultery as a comic theme were rare in English drama: it ran against the grain of romantic comedy because the genre typically worked towards the establishment of a stable family unit in marriage. When it appeared as a theme in drama, it was usually as one of the destructive circumstances of tragedy: it is at the root of *Arden of Faversham* (anonymous, 1590), for example, in which the wife seeks to end her superseded marriage through murder; the play demonizes her not only as a response to her criminality but to her sexual infidelity too. What Chapman recognized was that the marital anxiety underlying such scenarios could be funny, particularly if the feared event never actually happens: in *The Blind Beggar* it is literally impossible, because the adulterer is also the cuckold. *The Comedy of Humours* is if anything even more lubricious in its sexual humour (one of the pranks centres on a supposed threat to cut off a character's penis), but again the jealous spouses have nothing to worry about: Lemot may tempt the devout Countess, exposing the hidden promiscuity which the Elizabethans often suspected lay beneath religious zeal, but it is only to teach her a lesson about wifely chastity. Her husband's suspicions, and those of the old wife who will not let her young husband even look at another woman, are funniest because they are unfounded.

So 1597's summer craze for *The Comedy of Humours* probably focused on three novel elements of the play, two of which had been anticipated in *The Blind Beggar* the year before: its realistic setting, its sexual content, and its comic characterization in terms of specific personal eccentricities or 'humours'. All of these were to become standard features of the genre for the next decade and more. Contemporary England, and in particular London, became a popular location for comic events, with precise topographical references defining the characters' movements and misunderstandings. The earliest surviving London comedy is William Haughton's *A Woman Will Have Her Will* (later published as *Englishmen for My Money*), written for the Admiral's Men during the spring of 1598. It includes a bustling scene in the city's trade centre, the Exchange, and a farcical nocturnal sequence which depends on the familiar layout of its streets. The plot deals with the competition between Englishmen and foreigners to marry the three daughters of a wealthy usurer, and the sequence in question turns on the fact that the foreigners don't know their way around London in the dark, and so are easily misdirected by their home-grown rivals. The resolution of the plot, in which, predictably, the father wants wealthy foreign sons-in-law and the daughters want sexy English husbands, also illustrates the genre's startling new frankness: whereas, in *A Midsummer Night's Dream*, Hermia had insistently told her boyfriend to 'Lie further off' (2. 2. 50), in Haughton's play one of the English suitors uses pre-marital sex (and, it is suggested, preg-nancy) as a way of forcing the father's hand.

Unusual sexual situations became part of comedy's stock-in-trade, and a number of characters are defined by their deviant sexual prac-tices. In *Every Man out of His Humour*, Jonson anticipated Pinter's *The Lover* (1963) by centuries in portraying a man who enjoys play-acting adultery with his own wife, in scenarios drawn from the chivalric *locus classicus* of the Lancelot and Guinevere story. It is possible to see a sensitive treatment of female masochism in Shakespeare's portrayal of Isabella in *Measure for Measure* (1604) and Helena in *All's Well That Ends Well*, while Jonson is more robustly aggressive in his presentation of male proclivities like Nick Stuff's clothing fetish in *The New Inn* (1629), or Corvino's nasty taste for anal rape in *Volpone* (1605–6): 'no pleasure | That thou shalt know,' he promises his unwilling wife, 'but backwards' (2. 5. 60–1). The plays often portray a London full of predatory courtesans and louche sex-seekers, along with their inevit-able corollary, jealous husbands like Thorello in *Every Man in His Humour* (who later became Kitely when Jonson revised the play to give it a London setting); in Thomas Dekker's *The Triangle of Cuckolds* (1598, lost), 'cross-wooing' probably turned into cross-adultery in a circular sequence of extra-marital intrigues. One of the most prolific writers of this kind of comedy, Thomas Middleton, also had a peculiar fascination with the converse situation of the wittol, a husband con-tent to prostitute his own wife in return for material rewards and freedom from her sexual demands: such figures appear in both *The Phoenix* (1603–4) and *A Chaste Maid in Cheapside* (1613) as well as in several of his tragedies.

In many cases these sexual peculiarities are a sub-species of the 'humours' which increasingly dominated comic characterization after Chapman. Romantic comedy had tended to ring humane changes on a limited group of stock types inherited from Roman and Italian drama:

lovers and misers, clowns and braggarts, foolish fathers and cheeky pages. Compared with these, 'humours' roles can look narrowly caricatured in their focus on a single dominant trait; yet they also opened the genre to a tremendous range of human experience. When, in the prologue to *Every Man in His Humour*, Jonson proclaimed a great advance in character realism, it was no idle boast. Now all kinds of people featured in comedies. People who are predisposed to a particular mode of behaviour, like the excessively uxorious Deliro in *Every Man out of His Humour* or the excessively pugnacious Giuliano (in the revised version, Squire Downright) in *Every Man in*. People with some bizarre, fanatical fixation like Morose in Jonson's *Epicoene* (1609), whose manic desire for silence causes him to sound-proof his house with mattresses. People who won't stop talking, like Carlo Buffone in *Every Man out of His Humour*, who ends up having his mouth sealed with wax, and people who won't talk at all, like Granuffo the silent lord in Marston's *The Fawn* (1605). People who talk in an egregiously odd way, like Nicholas the servant in Henry Porter's *The Two Angry Women of Abingdon* (1598), who speaks nothing but proverbs. Much more of human life is here than there ever was in the comedies of Lyly and the early Shakespeare.

The figure who was almost left behind by these developments was the company clown. Of course, roles were still being written for such performers: Porter's Nicholas is one, and another is Dogberry in *Much Ado About Nothing* (1598), with his 'humour' of persistent malapropism. But the typical clown part had become virtually incidental: a character who counterpoints the main action's romanticism with his down-to-earth attitudes, and who is funny in himself rather than in the situations he encounters, is rather less useful in a realistic comedy which takes as its premise the assumption that everyone is inherently humorous (in both senses of the word). In *The Two Angry Women of Abingdon*, Nicholas is as detachable a comic turn as Lance had been in *The Two Gentlemen of Verona*, but with none of the meaningful contrast: he is largely there not for artistic reasons but to give the clown something to do. Shakespeare tried to integrate the character by giving Dogberry an unwonted degree of narrative responsibility: in arresting and interrogating Don John's accomplices, he and his colleagues play a crucial part in unravelling the plot. But it seems to have been Chapman who devised the problem's most original and influential solution.

Here we must be tentative. Chapman continued to work for the Admiral's Men for two years after *The Comedy of Humours* until one of the new boy companies snapped him up, but none of the plays he wrote for them during that time has survived: we have to speculate about the output of London's most fashionable comic playwright from the cryptic titles recorded by Henslowe in his account-book. His last Admiral's comedy, written in the summer of 1599, gives us the easiest guess: it was called *All Fools but the Fool* (not to be confused with his later, surviving, boy-company play, *All Fools*). The title seems to be saying that the comedy is based on a neat paradox: all the characters are foolish, except for the one who is a fool (and who would be the obvious role for the company's principal clown). Exactly what kind of fool we shall never know. Chapman may have been thinking of Dogberry's pivotal role in *Much Ado About Nothing*, which focuses a similar incongruity articulated by one of the miscreants: 'What your wisdoms could not discover, these shallow fools have brought to light' (5. 1. 225–7). He may, too, have remembered the proverbial notion that fools always told the truth, which Haughton had mentioned in the second scene of *A Woman Will Have Her Will*. But it is also just possible that his unfoolish fool was not this kind of unwittingly able idiot but a professional jester, the original of the 'wise fool' character who starts to appear in Shakespeare's comedies with *As You Like It* the following year, using his folly as a stalking-horse to conceal the barbs of his wit; and who would eventually undertake his most serious fooling in *King Lear* (1605).

Romantic Humours and Comical Satires

Jonson and Shakespeare dealt with the change in comedy in characteristically different ways. Shakespeare's first response to Chapman's innovations—perhaps the first by any dramatist—was *The Merry Wives of Windsor* (1597–8), in which Falstaff's associate Nim enthusiastically throws about the fashionable new buzz-word, 'humours'. With its loose intrigue plot, independent comic set-pieces, and English setting defined by specific local reference, it is an anomaly among Shakespeare's comedies which is sometimes explained with reference to another of Nicholas Rowe's legends, that it was written in response to the Queen's command for a play showing Falstaff in love. The truth or otherwise of that tradition is less important than the sense it articulates of an unusual external influence on Shakespeare's creativity; eighteenth-century *literati* may have been more inclined to look to royal patronage than to commercial competition as the source of that influence, but the insight was sound enough. Shakespeare was never entirely insulated from what other dramatists were doing (that is the whole point of this book), but *The Comedy of Humours* was so original and different that his initial riposte was quite unlike his usual style. The new fashion was then more securely assimilated in his next comedy, *Much Ado About Nothing*, which he must have been writing at the time Jonson offered the company *Every Man in His Humour.*

One respect in which *The Merry Wives* and *Much Ado* are like Chapman's comedy is the importance of human agency. The action takes place in unrelievedly domesticated settings like Leonato's private orchard or the streets of Windsor and Messina—even Windsor Park, where *The Merry Wives* reaches its arboreal climax, is actually an enclosed royal estate—and the events remain tightly under human control, created not by chance, still less by any supernatural force, but by the machinations, not always benevolent, of particular characters, from the genial, manipulative Host of the Garter to the melancholy Don John. 'We are the only love-gods' (2. 1. 361–2), says Don Pedro when he outlines his scheme to inveigle Beatrice and Benedick into open love with one another: a Lylian Cupid is not only absent but positively excluded. Both plays underline their human-centredness by invoking particular examples of Shakespeare's previous practice. The last time he had presented a friar advising a young woman to feign death, in *Romeo and Juliet*, it had all gone horribly wrong in a grand, tragic demonstration of the intractibility of real life; but in *Much Ado About Nothing*, Friar Francis (a character whom Shakespeare did not find in the play's narrative source) achieves the happy ending that Friar Laurence had fumbled. As for *The Merry Wives*, Falstaff's journey into the forest entails his meeting fairies and being 'made an ass' (5. 5. 118); but though they are just as much the shock troops of monogamy as their predecessors in *A Midsummer Night's Dream*, these are no woodland spirits, only costumed schoolboys.

The eighteenth-century myth makers were astute to home in on Falstaff in love as a focus for their sense of influence, in part because, like its successor, *The Merry Wives* exploits the new fashionableness of sexual themes in its attempted-adultery scenario. The title *Much Ado*

About Nothing, too, is not just a wry acknowledgement of the new unimportance of plot, nor only a punning reference to the action of observing, or 'noting', other characters' foibles; it is also one of Shakespeare's smuttiest *double entendres*. If the story is about anything at all, it is much ado about vaginas, also signified by the word 'nothing': women's chastity is the centre of male anxiety, particularly, though not exclusively, in the strand about Claudio and Hero. Both these plays, like *The Comedy of Humours*, are deeply concerned with the manic 'humour' of sexual jealousy and the antisocial behaviour it induces.

More particularly, though, Falstaff in love is a character paradox: it is a Falstaff who is not Falstaff, or at least not the seedy, sack-sodden, and strangely endearing coward of the *Henry IV* plays. But in this respect it is a device which aligns him with a species of 'humours' characters who try to be what they are obviously not, like the would-be poet Matheo (in the revised version, Matthew) in *Every Man in His Humour*, who turns out to have plagiarized his verses from Marlowe and Samuel Daniel. The fat knight's 'humorous' notion that he is constantly being ogled by attractive women is a common male fantasy, but in his case it is not only unfounded but ludicrous: even Nim and Pistol can see that he could never be sexually attractive to women, and that he is just projecting his own erotic fantasies onto Mistress Ford and Mistress Page. The comic action is unusually character-driven in that it unfolds out of the mismatch between those fantasies and the reality of the wives' robust common sense.

Shakespeare went on to develop an even more elegant example of such perverse 'humours' in *Much Ado About Nothing*. Many romantic comedies feature unrequited love as part of their 'cross-wooing' action, with one half of the couple spurned by the other: Helena and Demetrius in *A Midsummer Night's Dream*, for example, or even Petruccio and Katherina in *The Taming of the Shrew*. The more memorable of *Much Ado*'s two pairs of lovers, Beatrice and Benedick, take this a step further in that they both do the spurning. It is a conceit typical of the simple, metallic logic that underlies most of Chapman's comedies; but, like the play's sexual content and its human-centredness, it is much more securely assimilated into Shakespeare's familiar romantic mode as the narrative takes its usual course from emotional upset to eventual happy marriage. *Much Ado About Nothing* is his most accomplished attempt at a 'humours' comedy, but it is telling that nobody has ever thought it unShakespearian in its style or felt the need to explain it away with a legend about its origins.

So Shakespeare responded to Chapman's new style of comedy by absorbing it. As the less established and less experienced dramatist, in contrast, Jonson's impulse was to totalize it: Chapman had written about a range of characters with funny quirks and affectations, but Jonson topped him with a play in which *Every Man* was *in His Humour*. As the most intellectually self-conscious playwright of his time, he then attempted to theorize 'humours' characterization in *Every Man out of His Humour*, which uses the device of an on-stage audience who keep up a running commentary on the play as a work of art. He had little patience with the kind of externalized eccentricity that Henry Porter had used in *The Two Angry Women of Abingdon* with Nicholas and his folksy proverbs: one of the characters complains of how, now that the word 'humour' has become fashionable, it is being misapplied to every silliness and idiosyncrasy, so that 'if an idiot | Have but an apish or fantastic strain, | It is his humour' (ind. 115–17). Jonson held that the word should be more strictly defined in terms of its contemporary medical sense, which referred to the four fluids of the human body, blood, bile, melancholy, and phlegm; it was believed that a person's character and temperament were determined by the proportions in which these fluids were mixed, so that, for instance, an excess of physical melancholy would cause psychological melancholia. Shakespeare seems to have interpreted this literally, writing a sequence of references into *Much Ado About Nothing* which frame the action as a contention between the sanguine and melancholic humours. But for Jonson, the concept's application to dramatic character was metaphorical:

> when some one peculiar quality
> Doth so possess a man, that it doth draw
> All his affects, his spirits, and his powers,
> In their confluctions, all to run one way,
> This may be truly said to be a humour.

> (induction 105–9)

In other words, a character's 'humour' was not just a quirk but an obsession, a psychic imbalance comparable with Renaissance medicine's conception of mental illness.

Though it has little discernible plot, *Every Man in His Humour* still has an obviously comic *process*: its events lead up to Lorenzo Junior's marriage to Hesperida (in the revised version, Edward Knowell's to Bridget), and the characters ultimately gravitate together for a concluding, festive dinner at Doctor Clement's house. In *Every Man out* there is a greater sense of loneliness and harshness. At one point a member of the on-stage audience comments that the characters might have appeared individually rather than in groups, so isolated are they by their 'humorous' obsessions, and the ending brings them no happy confluence, only humiliation and grief: Puntarvolo is left mourning for his dead dog and Deliro is convinced that his beloved wife has cuckolded him, while the courtly poseur Fastidius Briske can only look forward to a lifetime rotting in a debtors' prison with little prospect of paying back the £13,000 he owes. When he published the play in 1601, Jonson pointedly did not call it a comedy but a 'comical satire'.

Dramatic historians often point to 1599, when Jonson wrote *Every Man out of His Humour*, as the year when the stage became a vehicle for satire. They attribute the change to a forced migration of literary satirists into the theatre after the authorities cracked down on printed books that summer. This certainly fits the career of John Marston, whose verse satires were among the volumes burned by the public executioner in June, and who appears in Henslowe's records as a new playwright early that autumn; but as a general statement it is far from accurate. It is likely that Chapman was already writing satirically (his lost 1598 play, *The Fountain of New Fashions*, can hardly have been otherwise), and in any event there was a long tradition of satirical themes dating back to the old morality plays, which many years later Jonson was to call England's 'old comedy'.[3] In the later years of its existence the genre shed many of its metaphysical trappings to concentrate on contemporary social abuses in plays like *The Three Lords and Three Ladies of London* (Robert Wilson, 1588), *The Cobbler's Prophecy* (Wilson, 1590), and *A Knack to Know a Knave* (anonymous, 1592): the devilish jollity of figures of supernatural or allegorical evil gave way to the actual wickedness of dishonest tradesmen, grasping landlords, and corrupt usurers, and the eternal torment of hell was supplanted by gruesomely physical punishments in this world (*A Knack to Know a Knave* has some of the nastiest, involving eyes being pecked out). Such 'morals' had all but died out in the late 1590s, perhaps because the other genres, and particularly comedy, were taking over their characteristic material. For comedy, the crucial year was not 1599 but, once again, 1597.

Two summers before the bonfire of printed satires, the authorities gave order for the closure and demolition of London's playhouses. It was a measure seemingly taken in rage, and soon thought better of: the theatres remained standing, though they did not reopen until the autumn. The trigger was *The Isle of Dogs*, a comedy written by Jonson in collaboration with Thomas Nashe, whose content struck the Privy Council as lewd, seditious, and slanderous; nobody knows for certain what that content might have been, for understandably the text does not survive, but the play was obviously satirical. It is significant, however, that the impulse was to punish theatre as a whole rather than just the company and authors responsible for the particular offence. *The Isle of Dogs* was the flashpoint, but it arose out of the broader dramatic temper of the year, which also saw the vogues for 'humours' and for guying Marlowe.

'Humours' characterization is always to some degree satirical, because it assumes a critical distance between character and spectator. This is the import of the jealous remark Jonson puts into the mouth of the poetaster Antonio Balladino who appears in the revised version of *The Case is Altered* (*c*.1601; originally written in 1597):

> you shall have some now (as for example in plays) that will have every day new tricks, and write you nothing but humours. Indeed this pleases the gentlemen, but the common sort they care not for 't; they know not what to make on 't; they look for good matter, they, and are not edified with such toys. (1. 2. 60–5)

We have no way of knowing whether the 'humours' craze really was a gentry fashion not shared by more plebeian spectators, but as a mode of character writing it gave audiences the superior vantage-point associated with social privilege. *Tamburlaine the Great* had empowered playgoers through their identification with the aspirant hero as he shears through society's established boundaries. *The Comedy of Humours* did the same by disengaging them from its characters, among them a king and queen: the people on stage are funny because in their bizarre fixations they are presumed to be lesser than the people watching them from the auditorium. Chapman's play was not in itself an egregious offence to authority, but it was certainly a major step on the way to the presumed sedition of *The Isle of Dogs*, and beyond that, to *Every Man out of His Humour*.

However, it is as well to remember that Jonson's play is not only a satire, a portrait gallery of obsessives held up for criticism and mockery, but also comical. In this respect its opening disquisition on the theory of 'humours' is important. In the late 1580s and early 1590s, satire and comedy shared a fundamental concern with equilibrium, which also differentiated them from the tragedies of the time. In satire, it is taken to be the basic principle of a just and ordered commonwealth: all the estates of the realm should exist in mutual interdependence with one another, and people who pursue their own ends to the exclusion or detriment of others are stigmatized as morally errant forces ripe for punishment. Obversely, comedies celebrate equilibrium's emergence from the welter of life's chaos and entropy, with disorderly situations cultivated in order that they may be set right at the end. And in Jonson's definition, 'humours' characters are themselves suffering from a psychological disequilibrium which is not only to be satirically exposed but also comically purged: every man must not only be ridiculed for the sake of what Jonson calls 'the correction of manners' (3. 6. 208–9), but also eventually put out of his humour. In that sense the play has, at its deepest level, as comic a process as its more genial precursor.

Jonson is often accused of sadism towards his characters, in open or implicit contrast with a generosity of spirit attributed to Shakespeare: we may think of Volpone, sentenced to prison shackles until he truly has the mortal illness he merely feigned in the course of the play; or the bad poet Crispinus, Jonson's stage caricature of Marston, forced to vomit up his hard words into a basin at the end of *Poetaster* (1601); or harmless, silly Dapper in *The Alchemist* (1610), locked in the privy and choking on his gingerbread gag. Yet it would not be difficult to point to corresponding examples of Shakespearian sadism: Sir Andrew Aguecheek's bloody head at the end of *Twelfth Night*, say, or the psychological torture meted out to the blindfolded Paroles in *All's Well that Ends Well*. There is a complicatedness to Jonson's aggression, however, which is well illustrated by *Epicoene*'s brief epilogue: 'Spectators, if you like this comedy, rise cheerfully, and, now Morose is gone in, clap your hands. It may be that noise will cure him, at least please him.' The courtesy of having waited to applaud until the noise-hating Morose is safely off the stage is undercut by the assumption that he remains in earshot; yet loud clapping is still presented as an act of kindness towards him. In reality it will cure 'Morose' by changing him from the dramatic character into his own person, the actor playing the part, who will be pleased and not perturbed by the sound. (Does the performer come back on stage as himself and take a bow? Jonson does not tell us.) Yet it is also significant that Jonson should think in terms of curing Morose at all, and that the agent of the cure should be the thing he most detests. There is a sense of being cruel to be kind here, of a purgative process which is literalized in the emetic ending of *Poetaster*. It is never pleasant for any man to be driven out of his humour; it is indeed a process that is often nasty, painful, and protracted, but nevertheless one that is also necessary for his future mental health.

In their different ways, both Jonson and Shakespeare contributed and responded to the great extension of range that was the principal factor in comedy's progress during the last decades of the sixteenth century. The new realism, in settings, events, and characters, brought with it a vast array of kinds of experience hitherto excluded or treated only tangentially, among them not only sex but even death—the King of France in *Love's Labours Lost*, Puntarvolo's dog in *Every Man out of His Humour*, and Ragozine in *Measure for Measure* all die in the course of the action. Not all of these experiences could easily be contained in the kind of tight comic structures that Lyly had woven. Even before Chapman and Jonson arrived on the scene, Shakespeare was beginning to strain against the neatness of romantic comedy's happy endings. In *A Midsummer Night's Dream* he gently raises the possibility that a father might not finally be reconciled to his daughter's matrimonial choice: Oberon's intervention resolves the 'cross-wooing', but Egeus continues to demand legal sanctions and finally has his parental authority not so much flouted as trumped by the higher power of the Duke. *Love's Labours Lost* ends without the usual marriage, and subsequent conclusions are usually made slightly uncomfortable by the existence of a character whom they cannot accommodate, like Shylock, or Jaques, or Malvolio; the last words spoken in *Much Ado About Nothing* are of the punishments in store for Don John. In their willingness to admit such uninclusiveness and such severity, both he and Jonson grappled with the central problem of comic realism: the difficulty of benevolence in an imperfect world.

4

Interlude: How to Write a Play

At the start of *Every Man out of His Humour*, an otherwise harmless member of the fictional on-stage audience wonders whether the play to come will be following the rules: 'the equal division of it into acts and scenes according to the Terentian manner; his true number of actors; the furnishing of the scene with Grex, or Chorus; and that the whole argument fall within the compass of a day's business' (ind. 237–41). This is typical of educated opinion of the time, which was reflected in new university plays as well as in theoretical writings and *obiter dicta*. Ancient Roman drama was the model: a properly written play would have the formal characteristics of the comedies of Plautus and Terence or the tragedies of Seneca. It would be written in verse, and would have five acts: more was considered 'tedious', fewer 'not sufficient'.[1] In a tragedy, the acts would be separated by passages of choric commentary by one or more figures distinct from the play's main action, in verse that was metrically different from that main action. The characters' speeches would tend to be long and declamatory, and their content would often be descriptive or analytical, though brisk line-for-line exchanges, known as stichomythia, were also used. Calamitous or violent events at the end of a tragedy would take place off stage and would be reported in detail by a lamenting messenger. Finally, the entire plot would represent a single action, as required by Aristotle; a few English critics also insisted that it should take place in a single location during a period no longer than a single day, in accordance with the pseudo-classical 'unities' formulated in 1570 by Aristotle's Italian commentator, Lodovico Castelvetro.

As in any period, theory and practice did not always coincide. The occasional six-act comedies and four-act tragedies of the Terence and Seneca canons testify to a flexibility in the ancient writers that was rarely endorsed by their sixteenth-century academic commentators, and in the contemporary professional theatre, which obeyed the laws of the marketplace more readily than those of art, there was an even greater latitude in the cause of telling a story effectively. To the dismay of the learned, commercial plays ranged freely across lifetimes and continents—'Asia of the one side [of the stage] and Afric of the other'—and even conflated the genres, 'mingling kings and clowns . . . hornpipes and funerals'.[2] Violence, which theorists considered too disgusting to be enacted, was represented on stage, not to gratify sadism but to give plays a power and authenticity which the mere words of a reporter could not match: audiences could actually see characters stabbed, shot, strangled, smothered, impaled, hanged, mutilated, and even, somehow, beheaded, the better to enhance the pity and terror which had characterized the impact of tragedy since the time of Aristotle. The five-act structure was far from universal and, although most plays were still written mainly in verse, dramatists were also beginning to experiment with the subtler rhythms of prose. In *Every Man out of His Humour*, a friend of the author's gives his neighbour's learned expectations short shrift: it is, he says, 'too nice' (i.e. finicky) to follow the scholarly rules too exactly (ind. 242).

Plotting and Theming: The Arrangement of Action

At one level, it was playhouse practice rather than playwright preference that determined the organization of a play's material into sequences of events. Plays performed at London's indoor theatres always had five acts, but this was at least partly for pragmatic rather than aesthetic reasons: with their socially superior audience, they may have had pretensions to literary 'correctness', but in any event they needed regular breaks in the action to allow trimming of the candles which lit the stage, while a musical interlude diverted the seated, and so relatively captive audience. In contrast, four intervals could have been disastrous in the outdoor amphitheatres, where plays needed to hold the attention of the promenading spectators in the pit, who could easily walk out, or do worse, if bored; the norm was an unbroken run of action from the first to the last scene. (The act-divisions which appear in some modern editions are generally not authentic.) That tradition gradually ended after 1608, when Shakespeare's company acquired the Blackfriars playhouse and moved indoors for part of the playing year: five-act plays became standard for England's premier company, even when they were performing at the open-air Globe, and over the next decade the fashion spread to the rest of the outdoor theatres. At last the commercial stage observed one tenet of neo-classical propriety.

What was faultiness to some was freedom to others, however. Without the regular interruption of act-divisions, dramatists were at liberty to develop longer stretches of action where appropriate, and to experiment with other ways of pacing and punctuating their plays. Events often fall naturally not into five acts but two or three movements or 'discourses', each focusing on a different stage of the plot or a different antagonist: Duncan, Banquo, and Macduff in *Macbeth*, for example, or Clarence, Hastings, and Richmond in *Richard III*; in the latter case each section also has a different king on the English throne. Without intervals to mark off the sections, a playwright had, if he wanted the audience to recognize the shift, to introduce some kind of punctuation into the action itself. One long-standing technique was to insert episodes which were unrelated to and generically distinct from the main action. For example, the early Elizabethan tragedy, *Cambyses, King of Persia*, represents a good king who degenerates into a wicked tyrant, and has a clear beginning (virtue), middle (decline), and end (vice) separated by comic scenes featuring lowly characters who take no part in the rest of the action. The play's publisher described it as 'a lamentable tragedy mixed full of pleasant mirth', a claim gently mocked by Shakespeare in Peter Quince's 'tragical mirth' of Pyramus and Thisbe in *A Midsummer Night's Dream* (5. 1. 57); and this kind of 'mongrel tragicomedy' was often stigmatized as the epitome of popular artlessness.[3] But the key lesson of *Cambyses* was that a brief shift into a perceptibly different mode of action could help audiences to follow a play's development.

The approved, literary method of dividing a play was to introduce a chorus, sometimes supplemented with the 'dumb shows' (mimed sequences) that were used in several Inns of Court tragedies after they were first introduced in *Gorboduc*. In popular drama, the chorus or 'presenter' was sometimes an anonymous person who might also speak the prologue and epilogue, as in *Henry V*, and sometimes a quasi-allegorical character like Ate, the classical personification of disaster, in *Locrine* (anonymous, *c*.1586); he might also be an author presumed to have written the material represented in the play, such as the historian Guicciardini in *The Devil's Charter* (Barnabe Barnes, 1606), the poet Gower in *Pericles*, or Time in *The Winter's Tale*. Such figures could be used, as in *Henry V*, to create a five-act structure within the uninterrupted performance, but equally often they served a less classical division into two, three, or four segments, and occasionally more; *Pericles* has as many as seven, growing progressively shorter as the story accelerates towards its redemptive climax.

There were also subtler, less self-conscious ways of marking transitions in the action. Sometimes characters, particularly those with no other function, might behave like a chorus without being explicitly identified as such—for example, the three citizens who discuss the political situation in a short scene (2. 3) between the first and second movements of *Richard III*, and who are never seen again. Sometimes the narrative might be suspended for a purely discursive scene like those separating the three movements of *Macbeth* (2. 4 and 3. 6), or one that develops at length a metaphor focusing the play thematically, such as the horticultural scene (3. 4) in *Richard II* (1595), in which the characters' remarks apply as much to government as to gardening. And sometimes the periodic reappearance of a distinctive character or theme might act as a subtle 'milestone', as the Soothsayer frames the first movement of *Antony and Cleopatra* (1606), and the Fortinbras sub-plot appears at all the crucial structural junctions of *Hamlet*.

Of course, casting narrative material into dramatic form did not only entail dividing it into sections. Most of what we know about the complex process of composition has to be inferred from its end product, the plays themselves. It is clear that the scholarly ideal of a play exercised only a limited influence on professional dramatists; but a different, and less easily quantifiable area of their academic training was far more important. Most of them would have studied rhetoric as part of their grammar-school curriculum; Stephen Gosson and John Lyly also attended lectures on the subject given by John Rainolds at Oxford in the 1570s. As it was taught in the period, the process of rhetoric began with *inventio*, the finding out of the raw material for a speech, and it ended with the speech's delivery before an audience; between the two came what we would consider the act of composition proper, the stages of disposition and elocution, in which the structure and words were established. This is strikingly analogous with the gestation of a play: the dramatist would find his source material, then compose a 'plot' for approval by the acting company, giving a scene-by-scene breakdown of the action, a list of characters, and possibly other information. (The only surviving example, dating from the late 1620s or 1630s, includes detailed background notes on the geographical setting.) Then he would write the characters' speeches, and finally, as in rhetoric, the completed work would be performed.

The study of rhetoric gave authors an instinct not only for the order of composition but also for the arrangement of materials. Schoolboys learned techniques of sequence and digression, repetition and balance, comparison and juxtaposition; they learned how to manipulate listeners by varying the amount of time given to a particular point, by introducing the unexpected, and by escalating to a climax. And what rhetoricians did with words and sentences, playwrights did with characters and scenes. John Lyly, the pioneer of the euphuistic prose style in which everything 'hath his contraries', was one of the first to apply the mechanisms of rhetoric explicitly to plotting and structure as well as to language.[4] In the epilogue to *Sappho and Phao*, he describes the comedy as 'a labyrinth of conceits, divers times hearing one device'; but in all his plays the labyrinth is ordered by principles of parallelism and symmetry. Characters come in contrasting pairs or in numerically equivalent groups; plot devices balance each other—sleeping and waking, disguising and undisguising, enchantment and disenchantment—in order to open and close narrative possibilities; and these correspondences are underlined in structurally analogous groups of scenes.

For example, the main plot of Lyly's *Gallathea* begins with two shepherds, both concerned about their country's quinquennial practice of sacrificing the most beautiful female virgin to appease Neptune's wrath, each deciding independently to protect his daughter by disguising her as a boy. Each girl responds to her disguise in the same way, first with modest embarrassment, then by taking the other as a 'male' role model, and finally by falling in love with 'him', expressed in a pair of consecutive soliloquies (2. 4–5). The dominant rhetorical figure is paradox, not only in the much imitated device of the female boy but also, more broadly, in the comedy's orderly disorder, which is ultimately resolved by divine intervention and the metamorphosis of one girl's gender so that the action can conclude with the intersection of its parallel lines.

In the work of later playwrights, this kind of overt artfulness in the disposition of material tends to serve more particular ends. In *Love's Labours Lost*, with its King of Navarre and Princess of France, three attendant lords and three attendant ladies, wooing seems almost a function of arithmetical necessity; but in fact it all ends, 'not . . . like an old play' (5. 2. 860), with marriages deferred and the frivolous men brought to a graver sense of the seriousness and the responsibilities of love. The euphuistic balance of the character groupings helps to create an expectation which it is the comedy's purpose to frustrate: outside Lyly's world of Ovidian fantasy, stable resolutions are not so easily achieved. In tragedy, a genre less committed to equilibrium, plays are often structured around the significant repetition of events. Marlowe's *Edward II* (1592) exploits antithesis, for example: incidents from early in the action recur towards the end in inverted form, as the crimes of the King are re-enacted as crimes against the King, culminating in the terrible symbolic buggery of his murder. There is a looser pattern of repetition in *Richard II*, but again events tend to happen twice over— gages being thrown down, Richard 'descending' to talk to Boling-broke, the banishment of murderers whose crimes have benefited the crown—in a way which encourages comparison between the two main players in the deposition at the tragedy's political and imaginative centre.

These examples illustrate that a play's themes were as much a part of its structural make-up as was its story: the 'rhetorical' patterning of the action contributes not only to the play's narrative exposition but also to the audience's apprehension of its conceptual argument. Learned opinion, which usually considered the 'argument' of a play to be synonymous with its plot, did not grasp this principle until well into the twentieth century, and plays with multiple narratives were accordingly censured for their perceived failure of dramatic integration. In practice, however, paired plots often fulfilled the same functions of analogy and contrast, reiteration and emphasis, as paired scenes.

Sometimes the correlation between narratives is overt, as in *The Taming of the Shrew*, where the two sisters' marital stories come together at the end of the play, and the virago turns out to be the more obedient wife than her younger, Daddy's-girl sibling: each plot complements and qualifies the other, so that the dramatic experience of the two taken together is fundamentally unlike their effect if seen in isolation. Sometimes, however, the relationship is subtler. In Middleton and Rowley's *The Changeling*, the tragic murder plot in the castle and the comic adultery sub-plot in the madhouse appear to have only the most perfunctory of story links, but the thematic and situational parallels are more important: the manoeuvrings within the main plot's dark love quadrangle are replayed in the sub-plot, with the asylum setting acting as a metaphor to focus the main-plot characters' degeneration from the norms of their civilized, rational society; the agent of that degeneration, their uncontrollable sexual feelings, is the principal constant in both plots.

Even a play which seems egregiously disjointed in its narrative may be held together by a central argument. For example, Samuel Rowley's Henry VIII play, *When You See Me, You Know Me* (1604), appears on the surface to be just a well-made episodic play (if that isn't a contradiction in terms): it presents not a unified, developing plot but a sequence of discrete incidents, with neatly layered transitions between them, in which the King variously receives ambassadors, arranges for his son's education, and undertakes, Henry V-like, a nocturnal, incognito tour of inspection around London. What makes the play more than its parts is the theme which recurs in them all: in each section, the King is shown in the act of government, whether at the level of European politics, home affairs, or as the head of his own immediate family, and through this he achieves a greater degree of personal control at the end of each sequence than he had at the beginning. This is an issue from the first scene, when Henry's foreign and religious policies are dominated by Catholic ecclesiastical interests, and in particular by Cardinal Wolsey: 'Great England's lord have I so won with words | That under colour of advising him | I overrule both Council, court, and King.' (121–3) The Cardinal's international activities, in which the overriding objective is to make himself pope, are clearly bound up with personal power rather than with England's advantage, as Henry recognizes at the end of the play when Wolsey's duplicity is exposed and his foreign policy collapses: 'Mother of God, if this be true, we see | There are more kings in England now than we.' (2968–9) The play's overall point about the power of the crown, then, is not made through a single developing action but through variegated repetition in a series of episodes whose apparent disconnectedness also emphasizes the range of different spheres in which royal authority must operate.

This is not to say, of course, that every dramatic gallimaufry of the time has some sophisticated principle of unity hidden within its disparate narratives. Some playwrights combined incidents with no more significant connection than their chronological proximity, occasionally using a presenter to stick together the less tractable bits. For instance, in Thomas Heywood's play about various events in Elizabethan history, *If You Know Not Me, You Know Nobody, Part 2* (1605, revised after 1625), the chorus makes his only appearance in order to waft the audience across three decades in a few disarming lines: 'From '58, the first year of her reign, | We come to '88, and of her reign | The thirtieth year.' (revised version, 2536–8) Some plays, moreover, explicitly offered anthologies of unrelated stories, occasionally interwoven but more often presented as sequential playlets within a framework: in the two-part *Seven Deadly Sins* (anonymous, *c*.1585, mostly lost), the poet Lydgate, as presenter, showed the imprisoned King Henry VI a series of short tragedies each illustrating one of the sins (lechery, naturally, being saved for last). The primary appeal of such plays, often with titles like *Four Plays in One*, seems to have been in the many plays rather than the one, in the individual narratives rather than the sketchy supra-plot which served as occasion for them.

There is some indirect evidence to support the view that audiences' conscious reception of plays tended to focus less on abstract issues than on plot, setting, and character: they attended to the story rather than the argument. By Shakespeare's time, a play's title, which some theatres displayed on a board visible on the stage during the performance, had become overtly part of its artistry. Some were simply descriptive, identifying the setting or central characters (*The Spanish Tragedy*, for example, or *Romeo and Juliet*), but since the 1560s proverbial phrases had also been used, pointing up significant thematic concerns: *Enough is as Good as a Feast*, *The Blind Eats Many a Fly*, *Measure for Measure*, *The White Devil*, and so on. Sometimes familiar sayings would be adapted to suit the play: 'labour lost', meaning wasted effort, is given added precision in the title of Shakespeare's comedy of unsuccessful wooing, *Love's Labours Lost*. Titles could also function as a comment on a play's dramatic construction, pulling focus onto a key type of recurring event (*The Comedy of Errors*, or *Love's Metamorphosis*) or an unexpectedly important feature of the narrative: the wise woman who is the title character of Lyly's *Mother Bombie* is the smallest named role, but it is also her prophecies that finally untangle the action. For audiences, however, titles seem to have been rarely more than labels with a far more straightforward relationship with the plays they identified: seventeenth-century people remembered *King Henry VIII* rather than *All is True*, *Malvolio* rather than *Twelfth Night*, *Vittoria Corombona* rather than *The White Devil*. The portrayal of distinctive major characters seems to have been a fundamental part of drama's appeal.

Dramatic Character and Dramatic Speech

For dramatic theorists, character writing was a relatively simple matter. The genres required specific types: according to Stephen Gosson, 'gods, goddesses, furies, fiends, kings, queens, and mighty men' in tragedies, and in comedies, 'cooks, queans [whores], knaves, bawds, parasites, courtesans, lecherous old men, amorous young men'. The playwright's task was to see that the roles exhibited the traits conventionally associated with such figures: 'grave old men should instruct; young men should show the imperfections of youth; strumpets should be lascivious, boys unhappy, and clowns should speak disorderly'.[5] This approach tended to favour stock characters (particularly those, like the irascible patriarch, cheeky slave, and braggart soldier, which England had inherited from Roman comedy), but in practice the best dramatists gave their creations an individuality that transcended, and sometimes even contradicted, popular archetypes: Othello is introduced by Iago as a standard lustful Moor and swaggering soldier, 'Horribly stuffed with epithets of war' (I. I. 14), but turns out to be neither when he eventually makes his first appearance; some later comedies emphasized their concern with exceptional, unconventional qualities in oxymoronic titles like *The Honest Lawyer* ('S.S.', 1615) or *The Just Italian* (William Davenant, 1629).

In the professional theatre, various pragmatic considerations combined to create a tension between character individuation and stereotyping. On the one hand, it was commercially desirable not to offer a repertory of plays (and so of plots and characters) which were unduly similar to one another; but on the other, the parts had to be cast from an established acting company of limited size. (In the 1590s, for example, Shakespeare's company numbered ten principals, plus boys and hirelings.) These men had particular strengths and physical characteristics which some dramatists would have taken into account as they wrote. Although acting is a protean art whose best practitioners are able to assume widely different identities, generic similarities between roles as performed must have been unavoidable. In some cases, indeed, they would have been actively intended: in the pirated version of *Hamlet* published in 1603, the grumpy Prince complains to the players not only about clowns who speak more than is set down for them, but also about the predictable ones who only have 'one suit | Of jests' to add, whatever the play—a phenomenon which might be more charitably interpreted as deliberately giving the audience 'old favourites' in the manner of twentieth-century comics like Eric Morecambe or Frankie Howerd.[6] Within a play, however, audience recognition of individual performers, despite changes of costume and make-up, could be a problem given that company size dictated that parts were routinely doubled. Some plays capitalized on this by using significant rather than merely pragmatic doubling: the first version of the anonymous arcadian romance, *Mucedorus* (c.1591, revised c.1605 and c.1609), calls for the same performer to play the three most vicious characters, the personification of Envy (i.e. malice), the hired assassin Tremelio, and the cannibal Bremo, emphasizing the thematic connection between them as agents of destruction. It is possible, too, that an actor's performance of multiple roles in the same play was relished as a display of skilful virtuosity; but in any event the action would be a mere confusion if audiences did not recognize that the roles *were* multiple. It was imperative, then, for a play's characters, and especially its bit-parts, to be clearly individuated in relation to one another, however prone they might be to stereotyped traits shared with comparable figures in other texts.

Today we usually think of 'character' as something that starts inside, in the private subjectivity of the individual mind, and then manifests itself outside in words and actions. Character writing for the stage, however, works perforce in the opposite direction: the theatre can only portray what is visible externally, or can be made so. Since classical times it had been conventional to represent the unspoken by speaking it: characters would address the audience directly in soliloquies and asides in order to articulate secret thoughts and motives relevant to the operation of the plot. By the late sixteenth century, when humanist emphasis on the autonomous self-determination of mankind had led English culture and social institutions towards a greater attention to the secret internal spaces within human beings, dramatic characters had to meet new expectations of complexity and psychological depth. Superficiality, which might once have been common to most theatrical roles, had become explicitly a singular personal trait, sharply anatomized in Paroles of *All's Well That Ends Well*, a man of words without substance, or, as old Lafeu puts it, a 'light nut' with 'no kernel' (2. 5. 43)—the point being that his surface bravado does not reflect the worthless inner cowardice that is revealed as the action develops. A dramatic character now had an inside as well as an outside, and it had become axiomatic that those insides and outsides did not necessarily match: as King Duncan says in *Macbeth*, 'There's no art | To find the mind's construction in the face' (1. 4. 11–12). A number of plays turn on the exposure of such discontinuities between external seeming and actual character, whether through the agency of the accusing ghost in *Hamlet* or the more earthly manipulations of the Duke in *Measure for Measure.* Soliloquy accordingly grew from declaration to dynamism: characters no longer just stated their motives but actively reasoned them out, like Hieronimo in *The Spanish Tragedy* deciding to take revenge rather than trust to providence; while in *Doctor Faustus* the title character's agonized contemplation of eternal damnation illustrates how extremes of emotion could now be shown with an intensity and precision beyond the strict requirements of plotting.

Obviously not every character could be explored in the same detail, and in practice individuality was often as much a function of language as of psychological depth. Roles might have a distinctive verbal tic or expression, like Mistress Quickly's tendency to repetition when agitated—'Do your offices, do your offices, ... do me, do me, do me your offices' (*Henry IV, Part 2*, 2. 1. 40–2)—or regular asseverations like 'O Jesu' (Mistress Quickly again), 'Let that pass' (Mistress Eyre in

Dekker's *The Shoemakers' Holiday*), or 'Work upon that now' (Touchstone in *Eastward Ho*). Comic parts in particular were often characterized in this fashion, because of the humorous opportunities in the verbal devices themselves, but a catch-phrase could also sometimes turn serious: in *Guy, Earl of Warwick*, for example, Sultan Shamurath is initially marked out as a deluded pagan by his repeated prayer, 'And Muhammad direct my course aright', but this also serves in retrospect to set in relief his eventual conversion to Christianity by the hero.

From the earliest days of the London theatre, various forms of linguistic confusion were popular as sources of both character and comedy. Foreigners might speak pidgin English, like the comic assassin Jaques in Greene's *James IV* (1590), who makes his final exit from the play declaring, 'me will homa to France and no be hanged in a strange country' (5. 2. 23–4). Serious-minded theorists disapproved, thinking it 'against law of hospitality to jest at strangers because they speak not English so well as we do'; but even anglophone characters were not immune from such mockery.[7] Malapropism was a staple comic device centuries before Sheridan gave it a name, and more than a decade before Shakespeare created its ultimate exponent, Dogberry in *Much Ado About Nothing*. Often it was simply an opportunity to raise an easy laugh at a bawdy substitution, as when the Scythians become the 'Shittens' (729) in *Locrine*, or an ignorant reversal of meaning, as in *A Knack to Know an Honest Man* (anonymous, 1594), when a shepherd, giving evidence, declares that he will be 'forsworn' (188) to its veracity. This is not much different from laughing at funny foreigners: the joke works by placing the audience in a position of linguistic superiority that was often associated with a better education, so that, for example, we laugh at the braggart soldier in *Fedele and Fortunio* when he mentions the classical gods 'Juniper' (836) and 'Cuprit' (614), because we know he means Jupiter and Cupid. Used more extensively, it explicitly satirized uneducated or plebeian people's attempts to extend their vocabulary beyond their capacity to understand.

Friar Tuck comments apropos of such a character, Ralph, in *The Downfall of Robert, Earl of Huntingdon* (Munday and Chettle, 1598), 'O foul corruption of base palliardise [lewdness, knavery] | When idiots witless travail to be wise.' (843–4) Few responses are as ill-humoured as this, but the plays tend to maintain a sardonic awareness of how the clowns, in their eagerness to use rare words, succeed only in evacuating their lexical meaning and turning them into mere gesture: Balurdo in Marston's *Antonio's Revenge* (1600), having learned the 'very good words' (1. 2. 86) *retort* and *obtuse*, proceeds to use them at every opportunity, apposite or not. A reason for such behaviour, and indeed for the strength of Tuck's reaction to Ralph, may be inferred from the verbal adventures of Costard in *Love's Labours Lost*, who says that, of his two most recent acquisitions, *guerdon* is 'better than remuneration' (3. 1. 165–6). He means it financially, taking the two words to refer to the different amounts tipped by Biron and Don Armado, but it was also true in terms of rank. *Remuneration* comes from Armado, the man of 'fire-new words' (1. 1. 176), and derives from Latin; *guerdon*, from Old French, is a word of longer standing and is used by the aristocrat Biron. The two words illustrate in little the social difference between ancient lineage and grammar-school Latinity, old blood and new learning, and in so doing underline that such differences could be reflected in linguistic register as well as in the more concrete signifiers of status like clothing and largesse: a king might not speak quite 'in King Cambyses' vein', as Falstaff calls the overblown style of the early Elizabethan stage tyrant (in *Henry IV, Part 1*, 2. 5. 390), but aristocrat and peasant would have distinct vocabularies and syntax. Balurdo, whose origins in Bergamo mark him out as the Italian equivalent of a country bumpkin, is consciously trying to make himself acceptable at court by ignorantly aping its elevated language; it is the mark of a social climbing which some, Friar Tuck included, would have considered presumptuous.

Prosody was another tool available to the playwright. The late 1580s saw a metrical revolution in commercial stage writing, discussed in Chapter 2, and though this development meant that, at the start of Shakespeare's career, dramatists were writing in a relatively more uniform style than ten years before, it also made diversity potentially more meaningful: they could use the various alternatives to blank verse, including prose, to make particular artistic points. Contemporary audiences, especially those who had studied verse composition at grammar school, probably had a better ear than we do for such metrical changes. They could certainly hear rhyme, as we know not only from the comments of contemporary critics, but also in the way it is sometimes used for jokes: in *The Cobbler's Prophecy*, Ralph Cobbler coyly suppresses the rhyme-word when, wishing that his nagging wife would 'come out of door' so that he can beat her, he calls her 'thou arrant thou' (instead of 'whore'; 70–1); and later in Jonson's *The Staple of News* (1626) the characters have a recurrent, self-conscious concern always to get the rhyme right. And since they were audible, couplets were a handy instrument of rhetorical punctuation, used to mark the ends of scenes or to divide long blank-verse speeches into 'paragraphs' (the opening monologue of *The Spanish Tragedy* is a good example); while larger deviations from the norm could adjust the tone of a sequence or the delineation of a role.

Despite its comic potential, rhyme was also sometimes used to give a character gravity: the hero of *Thomas, Lord Cromwell* speaks progressively more of it as he rises from middle-class bookworm to statesman. When Menenius Agrippa uses complicated syntax and sedate Ciceronian periods to deflate the rebellious and impatient First Citizen in the opening scene of *Coriolanus* (1608), he clearly understands the principle that, in language, formality and artifice confer power; so long as rhymes were not silly or jingling, then, they would enhance stature. The more laconic artifice of short, rhymed verse lines often marks out characters who are either other-worldly, like Hymen in *As You Like It*, or unworldly, like the rhyming nuns of *The Merry Devil of Edmonton* (anonymous, 1603?):

> Bid your beads and tell your needs,
> Your holy avés and your creeds;
> Holy maid, this must be done
> If you mean to live a nun.

> (3. 1. 62–5)

When prose irrupted into verse plays, its less obviously structured rhythms signalled a loosening of formality and artifice which made it often the distinctive argot of rustics and servants, plebeians and lowlives. However, it could also create a relaxed, laid-back tone for characters of higher rank, as in the first Belmont scene in *The Merchant of Venice* (1596), in which Portia discusses her suitors, or the riotous banquet in *Tamburlaine the Great*, when the caged Emperor Bajazeth is fed with scraps from his conqueror's table, or, even more alarmingly, the chaotic onset of King Lear's madness. Both conventions inform the alternation between verse and prose in the court and tavern scenes of the two parts of *Henry IV*.

In form and content, speech is the conduit leading from the inner world of thought to the public space of the stage: it is the most important component of any drama which accepted the humanist location of character in that hidden world. But this was not the only way of thinking about human behaviour. *Doctor Faustus* may end with existential engagement, depicting the psychological suffering of the doomed hero as an end in itself; but it also invokes an older tradition in the good and evil angels who incite Faustus heaven- and hell-wards. According to a prominent strain of pre-Renaissance thought which still survived in Shakespeare's time, a person was not the autonomous, self-directing agent presupposed by the humanists, but the focus of a range of coercive influences—mental, physiological, and supernatural—which were understood to be prior to his will to action. In the theatre, this meant that the motivating forces in characters' behaviour were conveniently external, like Faustus' instigating angels, or else could be made so through allegorical personification. One major strand of earlier sixteenth-century drama, the morality play, represented the struggle of these forces to possess the soul of a central human figure, who was consequently represented as a passive, suggestible being, his psychological interior emptied into his environment. Changes of mind and of moral character could thus be depicted through changes in the figures on stage: in John Skelton's political morality, *Magnificence* (1515), the protagonist despairs and attempts suicide in the presence of Despair, then brightens after the intervention of Good Hope. This was a drama in which villainous company could literally be the spoil of you.

By the 1560s some new plays were using allegorical techniques to different ends. An important development was the emergence of a 'hybrid' drama in which personified abstractions appeared alongside 'real' human characters: the title role of *Cambyses, King of Persia* was a known historical personage, but the cast also includes such figures as Attendance and Diligence, Proof and Trial, or Murder and Cruelty, who generally function as unindividuated minor characters, and sometimes as a form of shorthand in order to speed up the unfolding action. The key mid-century change was in the nature of the relationship between protagonist and abstractions, and it is neatly symbolized in *Appius and Virginia* ('R. B.', 1560), when the judge Appius succumbs to temptation and, as the original stage direction puts it, 'Conscience and

Justice come out of him'. It is a complex moment at which the two conceptions of human character temporarily coexist: Conscience and Justice recall the moralities' externalized psychological forces, and they duly attempt to induce Appius to virtue; but it is clear from Appius' own words—'But out, I am wounded! How am I divided! | Two states of my life from me are now glided' (501–2)—that their 'coming out of him' signifies that they have ceased to be inherent, motivating elements in his character. He is later able to ignore the voice of Conscience, and Justice is explicitly an independent agent when he reappears at the end of the play: summoned by Appius to execute a corrupt judgement, he acquits the accused and instead pronounces sentence against the unjust judge. He is no longer an attribute of Appius out of whom he came, but a form of commentary signalling a moral reading of the conclusion he brings about: he is Justice, so his acts are necessarily just. In *Cambyses*, in contrast, some of the personifications retain significant connections with the protagonist's personal character: Cambyses employs an assassin named Cruelty because he is himself cruel. However, the play's initiating acts of will are clearly shown to originate in the central human character, inverting the morality tradition: the abstractions are presented as Cambyses' servants, the agents rather than the creators of his wishes.

The two modes of characterization are creatively juxtaposed in *Henry IV, Part 1*, which draws extensively on morality-play themes and conventions in its story of Prince Harry's Eastcheap education. For early audiences, familiar with the chroniclers' tales of the wild prince, the play's most unexpected moment would have come at the end of the second scene, when Harry speaks the play's first soliloquy. Up to that point, we judge the Prince, as the King his father does, in terms of the company he keeps: jesting Poins and dissolute Oldcastle (as Falstaff was originally named). It is a morality paradigm which the play develops explicitly in later scenes, casting Oldcastle as the disorderly 'misleader of youth' who tempts the prodigal son (Harry) from the paths of virtue: he is the 'old white-bearded Satan' (2. 5. 467–8) who was traditionally both the father of lies and the principal comic role in earlier Tudor drama. But Harry's soliloquy, which reveals a psychologically complex Prince with an agenda beyond mere riotous living, disrupts all the conventional ways of reading the scenario: his interior subjectivity makes him more than the wild prince of legend, and it also empowers him against the defiling danger of his base companions. In that independence lie the seeds of his eventual rejection of Falstaff.

The other convention of morality characterization, the personified abstraction, also remained legible in Shakespeare's time, though it had become relatively uncommon in its purest form. But the allegory had never been entirely so pure as it can now seem: it is possible to overstate the distinction between allegorical and 'realistic' characters, between Everyman and any man. Modern readers of morality plays are constantly aware of the abstract nouns which are the speech prefixes, but when embodied by actors these figures would have a different impact; several early sixteenth-century moralities, including *Youth* (anonymous, 1514) and *The Summoning of Everyman* (anonymous, 1519), were published with woodcuts illustrating characters from the play, but, except for Death, only the captions distinguish the figures from generic social types. Allegorical personification is almost always human as well as abstract: we should see not only elements in a debate but also concrete comic characterization. Jonson later wrote in *The Staple of News* that 'vices' still featured in seventeenth-century comedy; they were just 'attired like men and women o' the time' (2. intermean 16–17).

A few plays with strong satirical themes used explicitly allegorical figures for emphasis—in *A Knack to Know a Knave* it is Honesty who exposes the various instances of social corruption—but more often they served as presenter or chorus, like Rumour in *Henry IV, Part 2* or Time in *The Winter's Tale*, and did not mix with the 'realistic' characters. However, even primarily concrete figures could embody an abstract level of significance: 'Pride went before, Ambition follows him' (1. 1. 178), comments the Earl of Salisbury on the successive exits of Cardinal Beaufort and then Buckingham and Somerset in *Henry VI, Part 2*, and the use of abstract nouns creates a broader and more overtly thematic reference than if they had simply been called proud and ambitious men. Here the effect is momentary, but it could be more prominent in minor roles: it is no accident that Edward II should be betrayed by a mower in Marlowe's play, or that the apothecary from whom Shakespeare's Romeo buys his poison should be 'worn . . . to the bones' (5. 1. 41), a walking skeleton; both are portrayed as human characters with their own economic anxieties, but both are also powerful visual allusions to the allegorical figure of Death.

In these examples, the morality-style abstraction is invoked as a way of adjusting the balance between particular and general in order to draw attention to a character's dominant personal trait or wider thematic function. During the 1590s this was largely superseded by the more straightforward and more flexible technique, inherited from classical comedy, of giving characters significant or suggestive names rather than naturalistic ones. For example, it is apt that the more reliable of the two deputies in *Measure for Measure* should be called, after the scales of justice, Escalus, and that the sick knight in Marston's *The Fawn* should bear the name Sir Amoroso Debile-Dosso. (Knights were a popular target of early seventeenth-century stage satire, and dramatists revelled in giving them ludicrous names like Sir Gosling Glow-Worm, Sir Marmaduke Manyminds, or Sir Toby Belch.) Others took their names from their occupations, like Snug the joiner in *A Midsummer Night's Dream* or Compass the sailor in *A Cure for a Cuckold* (Webster and Rowley, 1624), or from their circumstances: the character who marries beneath him in Richard Brome's *The New Academy* (1635) is almost bound to be called Matchill. But names could also help to place a character in terms of a play's broader concerns: in *The Spanish Tragedy*, the key to controlling the Spanish empire is marriage to the Duke of Castile's daughter, who is accordingly named Bel-Imperia; *Twelfth Night*'s dynamic opposition between festivity and ill-will is memorialized in the names of their principal exponents, Feste and Malvolio; and in *Bartholomew Fair*, Justice Adam Overdo is, true to his surname, excessively zealous in his judicial role and has to be reminded that he is also 'but Adam, flesh and blood' (5. 6. 96–7), as human and fallible as the fairground people he condemns. Of course, there are exceptions such as Angelo, the deputy who is tested and found wanting in *Measure for Measure*, and whose name, with its connotations of a value both heavenly and numismatic, is ultimately shown to belie the inner man; but in his case Shakespeare is evidently playing against convention rather than using it.

The examples of Overdo and Angelo indirectly illustrate the principal limitation of using names as a tool of characterization. Many a role is saddled with a name which declares the character to be only one thing: Sir Innocent Ninny of Nathan Field's *A Woman is a Weathercock* (1609) will always be an innocent ninny. In other words, meaningful nomenclature could help in the exposition of character, but usually at the cost of simplifying the role and narrowing its potential range. Overdo has the advantage of two names, one overtly significant, the other seemingly naturalistic but also quietly suggestive in its allusion to the biblical father of all mankind, and the character develops as the implications of the latter are brought out. In this he is unusual. Sometimes a character might seek to disguise his true nature by changing his name, following the example of the personified sins in morality plays, but this could only be a temporary deception: the honourable-seeming Medice in Chapman's bitter comedy, *The Gentleman Usher* (*c.*1602), whose name recalls that of the ruling family of Florence, will eventually be exposed as the deceitful gypsy Mendice, both mendacious and mendicant, and as imprisoned by his real name as any allegorical figure of vice. Angelo, in contrast, keeps his name, but escapes its implications, because we are misdirected as to its function: it seems significant but proves eventually to be merely naturalistic, its ironic suggestion of exceptional virtue reflecting only the inapposite arbitrariness of reality.

Artifice and Authenticity

Angelo's journey across the divide between art and life raises the fundamental aesthetic issue underlying every aspect of the playwright's technique: the balance between the opposite poles of literariness and verisimilitude. Hamlet, the most eloquent spokesman for the educated view of drama, insists that it should 'hold . . . the mirror up to nature' (3. 2. 22), and in the perverse looking-glass of the antitheatricalists, we can see how authors in the commercial theatre were valued for creating the illusion of life. The medium often dealt in fantasy, and took liberties with fact: 'plays are no images of truth,' fulminated Stephen Gosson, 'because sometime they handle such things as never were, sometime they run upon truths, but make them seem longer or shorter, or greater or less than they were, according as the poet blows them up with his quill for aspiring heads, or minceth them smaller for weaker stomachs.' His objection is to the art of play-making, whether used to originate narrative or transform source material, in that its end-product was not literally coextensive with reality. It followed that playwrights were professional liars: 'he that can make the most notorious lie, and disguise falsehood in such sort that he may pass unperceived, is held the best writer'. This account, preoccupied with the moral imperative of truthfulness, elides the important distinction between deception and the consensual practice of fiction, but in essence it provides a fair reflection of the theatre's institutional priorities. And the criteria which marked out the best writer also held for the best actor: 'what we see him personate, we think truly done before us,' wrote the playwright John Webster. So all the different constituencies which expressed an opinion were agreed that plays should in some way represent reality; the point at issue was how it should, and could, be done.[8]

Taken literally, Webster's comment suggests a drama committed to an artful verisimilitude, one that seems, like Polonius, to use no art at all; but this was obviously not the case. Various forces impelled playwrights in the opposite direction: we have seen that literary theory called for the inclusion of formal elements—act-divisions, rhetorical reports of off-stage action, verse (blank or rhymed)—which emphasized a play's artifice rather than its reality; and if those demands could easily be ignored, the practical limitations of the theatre itself were unavoidable. Some things simply could not be physically portrayed: 'Our stage so lamely can express a sea | That we are forced by chorus to discourse | What should have been in action,' (4. 5. 1–3) the audience is sheepishly told in *The Fair Maid of the West, Part 1* (Heywood, 1604) when an overtly literary device perforce becomes the only available medium of verisimilitude. Language remained the most sophisticated technology of representation, so in commercial drama the illusion often lay not in how something looked but how it was described: on a stage without elaborate moveable scenery, it was mainly up to the dialogue to create any background setting that was considered necessary. 'Think, when we talk of horses, that you see them,' requests the prologue to *Henry V*; and words not only supplied what could not be shown but also compensated for the limitations of what was shown. The title character of *Tamburlaine the Great* makes his first appearance in the second scene of the play; then, in the third, there is an account of his physical appearance which runs for 23 lines (which would be just over a minute in performance). If this were only a description of what the audience had already seen, it would be supererogatory; the point is that it establishes Tamburlaine as 'a wondrous man' (2. 1. 32), superhuman and therefore beyond literal embodiment in the person of the actor playing him. In much the same way, we have to be told how horrible the witches look in *Macbeth*, or how diminutive the fairies are in *A Midsummer Night's Dream*—small enough to wear the 'enamelled skin' (2. 1. 255) shed by a snake—because such beings are beyond stage representation.

Of course, it would be disingenuous of us to expect these plays to follow standards of realism comparable with our own, which are powerfully shaped by film and television. English Renaissance drama is a stylized form throughout, and it is a mistake to think of playwrights being 'forced' by the limitations of their medium to use less verisimilar methods of representation in every case. In fact, part of the professional dramatist's freedom from the prescriptive dictates of neo-classical literary theory was the liberty sometimes to accept its restraints: Shakespeare chooses to portray the murder of the Princes in *Richard III* through after-the-event narration rather than by enactment, and to contain the chaotic, crazy-paving narrative of *Henry V* within the regularity of five acts marked out by a chorus. One reason for this was that, as we saw in the way playwrights used the devices of rhyme and metre, the relationship between different degrees and different kinds of stylization could create meaningful effects.

A good example is *Romeo and Juliet*, a play of especially elaborate artifice. Its plot is more than usually 'rhetorical' in being constructed largely out of parallel pairs of major characters: two fathers (Montague and Capulet), two male kinsmen (Benvolio and Tybalt), two older counsellors (Friar Laurence and the Nurse), and a brace of the Prince's kinsmen (Mercutio and Paris). Its language, too, is full of high-flown metaphysical conceits (when it was first published it was called a 'conceited' tragedy), and the prosody of the verse is exceptionally regular. Rhyme is frequent, often in complex schemes: the prologue, the chorus, and the first exchange of dialogue between the lovers (1. 5. 92–105) are all sonnets. What is striking, however, is how quickly this artifice breaks down. The intricate weave of the prologue's sonnet sets a tone, but the start of the action belies it: the Capulet servants speak in demotic prose. This is a recurrent effect in the play: the complexity of its rhetorical constructions are always being interrupted or forestalled. After Romeo and Juliet conclude their first sonnet in a kiss, they immediately set out on another, but this time they only reach the end of the first quatrain before the Nurse arrives to call Juliet back to her mother's side. And on a larger scale, the play opens and ends a first act with a chorus which then never reappears: it signals itself as a formal five-act tragedy, but then settles down into the less obviously constructed flow of uninterrupted performance.

Shakespeare's idea of using act-division in this way probably came from *The Spanish Tragedy*, in which Revenge and the ghost act as chorus, but are also continuously present on stage watching the action. Their periodic conversations every 400 or 500 lines establish a pattern, which is then violated: after their dialogue at the end of the second act they are silent for 1,200 lines (roughly an hour). The reason is less immediately obvious to a reader than to an audience: Revenge has fallen asleep. It is a clever conjunction of the literal with the allegorical: the character's inattention means that in the main action the villains seem triumphant and the virtuous despair, while in the framework the performance skips an act-division. Though every printed edition marks only four acts, the play is better understood as a five-act tragedy in which the third and fourth merge together in unbroken action: the overt literary structure temporarily collapses at the same time as events appear to have spun out of control. Revenge then wakes at the start of the final act and reasserts his dominance: in the main action, justice, and vengeance, are achieved.

Romeo and Juliet is different because there is no full restoration of the broken structure: the Prince's closing remarks can only rise to an attenuated sonnet of a single quatrain and couplet. In Kyd's play, literary artifice marks the control of the higher powers, which may seem to have slipped but which is always apparent in the end. In Shakespeare's, however, it is a symptom of human efforts to impose order on the world: just as the high style is never sustained, so the characters are always thwarted in their impulse to control their destiny. Life proves intractable: Juliet may insist that it is the nightingale and not the lark outside her bedroom window, and that Romeo can stay with her a few more hours, but saying so cannot actually make it true. Whenever anyone takes any kind of positive action to shape a situation, it ends up going wrong: when Capulet tries to restrain Tybalt from making a scene at the party, he only succeeds in breeding an antipathy to Romeo which results in the deaths of Mercutio and Tybalt himself; when he tries to force Juliet to accept the intended marriage with Paris, he actually pushes her into her desperate gamble with the sleeping potion; and Friar Laurence always makes things worse with his benevolent efforts to create something harmonious out of a messy situation. The play repeatedly enacts the point in the juxtaposition of its differing degrees of artifice.

It is worth noting, however, that this technique could also work the opposite way around. At the climax of *Titus Andronicus* (1591–2), after the hero serves the cannibalistic banquet and kills his daughter, the dialogue moves from blank verse into the play's only sustained passage of rhyme (5. 3. 47–65). But the effect is not to distance the action on stage, much as many an audience might wish it. Rather it creates a frantic, headlong quality as events rush towards the final concatenation of slaughter: the language takes on a life of its own, and the characters seem no longer to be entirely free agents, their lines partly chosen for them by the rhyme-words. This is an effect which is only possible because the rest of the dialogue is predominantly in blank verse (in plays written mainly in rhyme, the couplets often seem to slow things down). As with *The Spanish Tragedy* and *Romeo and Juliet*, the play works through the contiguity of relatively greater and lesser degrees of artifice; but what it makes clear is that the effect depends on the difference between the two rather than on any absolute value attributed to one or the other. In these plays which sought to be true to life, there was no necessary association between artifice and unreality: literariness could be a vehicle for verisimilitude. To misapply the words of the clown in *As You Like It*, the art of English Renaissance drama could still be true even when it was most feigning.

5

The Hermaphrodite of Genres

Polonius' long list of seemingly modular dramatic genres—'tragedy, comedy, history, pastoral, pastorical-comical, historical-pastoral, tragical-historical, tragical-comical-historical-pastoral' (*Hamlet*, 2. 2. 398–401)—was a more specific and more timely literary joke than is often recognized; for the integrity of the genres defined by Aristotle was the central issue in one of the major aesthetic controversies of late sixteenth-century Europe. This was occasioned by the Italian playwright Giambattista Guarini's attempt to combine tragic and comic events in a single play, *The Faithful Shepherd* (*Il Pastor Fido*), which had been nearly thirty years in the writing before it was first performed in Mantua in 1598. In many respects the play is standard comic material, with multiple mismatched lovers, an interfering father, and a young man who would rather hunt than woo; but there is a significant breach of decorum in the fourth act when one of the characters is wounded and another is sentenced to death. Guarini's critics considered this a vulgar error, but he insisted that he had intentionally used an amalgam of elements from tragedy and comedy to create the new, baroque genre of tragicomedy. From tragedy, it took 'its great persons but not its action, its verisimilar but unhistorical plot, its stormy emotions somewhat attenuated, its pleasure but not its sadness, its danger but not its death', while comedy provided 'laughter that is not lewd, its modest pleasures, its fictional knot, its happy reversal, and above all the comic order'.[1]

Guarini's play was translated into English in 1602 (an Italian text had been available since 1590), and a Latin version was performed at Cambridge soon after, but the rumbles of literary debate were audible in England before then. They were certainly heard by John Marston, who had an Italian mother and may have been bilingual; he began to experiment with genre in 1600 in a diptych of plays written for the boy company at St Paul's, *Antonio and Mellida* and *Antonio's Revenge*. The first is a comedy of love which obviously lies somewhere deep in the imaginative genetics of *Twelfth Night*: its hero, the Genoese prince Antonio, is washed up on the Adriatic coast after a shipwreck in which he believes his father has perished, and since, like his namesake in Shakespeare's play, he must not be found in this enemy territory, he adopts the self-protective expedient of cross-dressing. The play's background in a bitter war between Italian states provides the danger-ous circumstances which, as in any comedy, are joyously circumvented in a romantic conclusion, and the characters leave the stage with a hopeful couplet from Antonio: 'Here ends the comic crosses of true love; | O may the passage most successful prove.' (5. 2. 272–3) Yet the wish itself emphasizes the provisionality of an ending which also looks uneasily fragile: Piero, the unsympathetic Duke of Venice, has offered a reward for the head of Antonio's father, but his malice just seems to evaporate when Andrugio brings it himself, still firmly attached to his own shoulders. The second play then realizes the doubts inherent in such a resolution by starting with the entrance of Piero covered in Andrugio's blood: the mode shifts abruptly into tragedy, ironizing the other characters who still behave as if they are in the closing stages of a comedy.

Marston was writing at a time when London audiences were pecu-liarly attuned to issues in literary theory. *Hamlet*, written in the same year as the *Antonio* plays, is a case in point. Today we are so familiar with Shakespeare's tragedy that we are rarely surprised by the actors' arrival at Elsinore with their generically diverse repertory; but perhaps we should be. No such characters had appeared in any previous version of the Hamlet story that we know about, and indeed they do not obviously belong in the play's revenge narrative. They have a plot function, it is true, and a thematic relevance too: the Ghost's command has made Hamlet himself into an actor, forced to conceal his true intentions behind a *façade* of madness, and his principal opponent is an actor too, who smiles and smiles and is a villain. But the immediate effect of their arrival is to make the action stop for a few minutes, not once but twice, while the Prince first listens to a piece of dramatic recitation, with impatient commentary from Polonius, and then indulges in some amateur theatre criticism when he tries to tell the players how best to do their job. Later legend turned this into Shakespeare's own opinion on acting, and so made it the most narratively superfluous part of the play never to get cut in production; in its own time, however, it was part of the new tendency for plays to hold the mirror up not only to nature but to their own art.

One symptom of this trend was a change in the inductions and framing devices which sometimes introduced or enclosed a play. Until 1599, these often used allegorical characters like Tragedy or Truth to place the main action in terms of its genre or themes, while a handful treated that action explicitly as a performance and presented the fictional circumstances in which it was taking place, such as to justify a character's misanthropy in *James IV*, as part of a practical joke in *The Taming of the Shrew*, or as a court rehearsal in *The Downfall of Robert, Duke of Huntingdon*. Beginning with *Every Man out of His Humour*, however, inductions came to focus on the play's actual situation as a performance in a contemporary London commercial theatre. There are scripted roles for (fictitious) audience members, who might keep up a running commentary on the action as it develops, and for (often real) actors, who are shown worrying about their parts or indulging in petty rivalries: the real process of theatre and of theatrical criticism, however rudimentary, became part of these plays' visible foreground, rather than something which was elided in an art of illusion. Chaotic events behind the scenes would erupt onto the stage, as when the author steals the prompt-book in Marston's *Jack Drum's Entertainment* (1600) to make some last-minute revisions, while genial boy actors would struggle to please the widely divergent requirements of their adult patrons, like the three in John Day's *The Isle of Gulls* (1606) who respectively want to hear satire, bawdy, and bombast. Eventually the device turned into full-scale burlesque in Francis Beaumont's *The Knight of the Burning Pestle* (1607), when the on-stage spectators insist on taking over the performance and substituting their own, markedly more plebeian, choice of play and cast.

Perhaps the most striking phenomenon of this self-conscious phase of drama was the so-called 'War of the Theatres' in a run of comedies between 1599 and 1601 which contained thinly disguised and often insulting caricatures of specific contemporary playwrights. At one level, this was a stage version of 'flyting', an elaborate exchange of invective between authors which was enjoyed as a literary form in its own right. (Nashe had taken part in a famous example in his 1590s pamphlet war with Gabriel Harvey.) The conflict was primarily driven by the violently clashing personalities of Jonson and Marston, and it became so bitter that prologues started to come on stage wearing not the traditional black cloak but armour ready for a fight, 'in confidence | Of author's pen', as the prologue to *Troilus and Cressida* (1602) described them. But it also focused a serious intellectual interest in the social purpose of literature. Beyond the personal element of their satire, the comedies are about bad poets who trivialize their art, often by using it for sexual purposes: Crispinus (representing Marston) in Jonson's *Poetaster* takes up poetry to make himself attractive to women, Antonio Balladino (representing Anthony Munday) in the revised version of Jonson's *The Case is Altered* hires himself out to write wooing verses, and in Dekker's *Satiromastix* (1601) Horace (representing Jonson) persuades a woman to jilt her bald suitor by writing a poem on the glories of hair. It is striking, however, how much consensus and how little real debate there is between these supposedly contending plays: the authors may have taken one another as their real-life targets, but their ethical position is always the same, that literature should have more serious concerns than being a mere instrument in the mating game. In that sense the plays were trading on the spice of controversy rather than its substance; but what is most remarkable about them is that literary theory, not as an object of satire but a serious theme, should ever have been thought an appropriate subject for comedy.

Three specific circumstances, all dating from 1599, influenced this new stage fashion: the arrival of Marston in the commercial theatre, the emergence of Jonson as a recognized major dramatist, and the revival of the boy companies which had fizzled out at the beginning of the 1590s. Each of them was likely to promote a more literary kind of drama; together they were decisive. The boys, written into *Hamlet* as the 'little eyases' (2. 2. 340) whose success has forced the adult players to tour, catered in their expensive indoor playhouses for a socially select audience which at least liked to think itself a more sophisticated group of *literati* than the amphitheatre rabble. Jonson and Marston were bound to be their playwrights of choice, reflecting opposite ends of the literary spectrum. Jonson was most comfortable with estab-lished and academically respected forms: he never entirely got over the adolescent trauma of being withdrawn from school by his stepfather and forced to take up the humble trade of bricklaying, and throughout his career he hoped to be known for the learning and neo-classical literary correctness of his plays. Marston, in contrast, was the best-placed of all dramatists to encounter new modes of writing: he was a member of the Middle Temple, then an important centre of London's literary avant-garde. It is no surprise that he should have been the first to bring Guarini's innovations to the London theatre.

The Disguised Duke Plays

In late 1602 or early 1603, Marston followed up the *Antonio* plays with a full-scale tragicomedy written for the boy company at Blackfriars, *The Malcontent*. This is in many ways a better exemplar of the genre even than *The Faithful Shepherd*: for all his efforts to justify himself theor-etically, Guarini had really just included some darker incidents in a predominantly comic plot. *The Malcontent*, in contrast, bears more comparison with the popular Elizabethan tragedies of dynastic politics like *Richard III* and *Hamlet*: at its root is the deposition of a virtuous ruler and the progressive moral and sexual corruption of the state under the usurper, a process which enables the emergence of an even blacker traitor, Mendoza; the focus of the main narrative is his attempt to seize power by having the new Duke murdered. Against this tragic intrigue, however, there is a countervailing comic intrigue centred on the old, banished Duke, who has returned to court disguised as a railing satirist. In this respect, the initial, tragic situation is tempered by the gentler politics of comedy: in that genre, deposed rulers go into exile, like Duke Senior in *As You Like It*, whereas in tragedy their life expectancy tends to be shorter, as in Marlowe's *Edward II*. The plot then develops by empowering the comic elements over the tragic so that the play concludes with the usual restoration of order as the original Duke, Altofronto, claws back his throne in a palace coup. Thus what was initially presented as an ongoing tragic situation is ultimately reinterpreted as the kind of disruption that a comic plot will typically reverse: Mendoza grows progressively less important and less fearsome until finally he is too minor an irritation to bother executing, and can merely be kicked off the stage by the restored Duke. As Altofronto says, 'an eagle takes not flies' (5. 2. 195).

The Malcontent was one of the outstanding theatrical successes of its time; it was quickly appropriated by the King's Men, who hired John Webster to adapt it for the adult stage, and it remained in their repertory for more than thirty years. In the short term, it was followed by a prodigious run of dark comedies using its central plot devices of disguised dukes, political displacement, and averted murder; these included Middleton's *The Phoenix*, John Day's *Law-Tricks* (1604), and of course *Measure for Measure*. They are plays which initially resist generalization: the narrative material drawn from *The Malcontent* is common to them all, but they use it to a variety of different ends, ranging from the prodigal son theme of *Law-Tricks* to the curious combination of city comedy and political melodrama in *The Phoenix*. What they all latch onto, however, is the way Altofronto's disguise enables him to expose vices that would otherwise remain hidden, or at least unspoken. In part this is simply because his alter ego, Malevole the satirist, is treated as a bitter kind of court fool, licensed to rail; but it is also because this identity gives him a point of view and an access which are not available to him in the person of the Duke. Here and in *The Phoenix*, the court is imagined as a place where ambitious men lurk, showing an emollient face to those above them whilst awaiting the chance to bring their desires to treasonous satisfaction, and whose plots ultimately fail only because of a poor choice of hired assassin (to wit, the incorruptible disguised princes who are the plays' ethical touchstones). In *The Phoenix*, the city too is a riot of improper sexual and legal practices conducted in the mistaken but not unreasonable belief that they will never be spied out by the aloof eyes of authority. Rulers may be benevolent and morally sound, but their position also makes them ignorant of the very things they need to know if they are to make their virtue politically effectual. The point is made succinctly by Prince Phoenix's royal father: 'State is but blindness; thou hadst piercing art. | We only saw the knee, but thou the heart.' (5. 1. 178–9) The presence of power changes the appearance of purpose: that is why disguise and deception are necessary instruments of state.

In the epilogue to *Law-Tricks*, this characteristic theme of hypocrisy is explicitly associated with tragicomedy's duality of genre:

Who would have thought such strange events should fall
Into a course so smooth and comical?
Who would have thought such treachery could rest
In such a smooth and virtuous-seeming breast?

These plays which warn against trusting to appearances are themselves deceptive in their use of apparently tragic material. Both the geniality of Day's tone and the self-reflexiveness of his point are important, not least because the action often goes beyond the simple process of investigation and exposure dramatized in *The Phoenix*. 'What's open made to justice, | That justice seizes' (2. 1. 22–3), says Angelo in *Measure for Measure* after Duke Vincentio has left him in charge, admitting the existence of the kind of secret abuses that Phoenix discovers on his incognito tour of inspection. But the plays' rulers tend to be as much concerned with vice as a phenomenon in potential: like Milton, they define virtue as an active quality which must be proven through positive resistance to temptation, and their disguise gives them the opportunity to invent situations that will put people to the test and reveal, as Vincentio puts it, 'what our seemers be' (1. 3. 54). Altofronto's Duchess passes, comprehensively vindicating her reputation for chaste fidelity when she rejects Malevole's suggestion that she should remarry, but more often these experiments with human moral character end up luring a dormant depravity into open commission: power turns the bookworm prince of *Law-Tricks* into a dissolute reveller who squanders public money on his quirky fancies, and Angelo proves to be more subject to the dominion of the libido than he or anyone else ever suspected. Isabella puts her finger squarely on the problem when, pleading for her abuser at the end of *Measure for Measure*, she says, 'I partly think | A due sincerity governed his deeds, | Till he did look on me' (5. 1. 442–4). These vices only come into existence because the disguised rulers have created the situations which induce them.

The Malcontent is less difficult in this respect, not only because Altofronto is not the creator of the play's circumstances, but also because it establishes a strong ethical framework based on his statement that 'birth doth ne'er enrol | A man 'mong monarchs, but a glorious soul' (5. 2. 170–1): the state's legitimate ruler attests the correlation of his constitutional and his moral authority. Though the action teases the audience with the possibility that he might be tempted by the opportunities for subversion and vengeance which the situation offers him, it is by not following that course that he establishes that authority, and so his fitness to test and judge others. The play is organized around a tripartite political hierarchy of actual and potential dukes, which is also a moral hierarchy, descending from Altofronto through the fallible but not irredeemable usurper Pietro to the outright villainy of Mendoza. (Some years later, in 1611, Shakespeare used the same three-tier structure in *The Tempest* to define the relative positions and worth of Prospero, Alonzo, and Sebastian, and invoked the same doubts about Prospero's ultimate intentions.) Altofronto's reign is portrayed as an admirable period of ethical rule which rotted away to sexual corruption when he was deposed: his regime had 'almost brought bed-pressing out of fashion' (5. 1. 53–4), says the bawd who has subsequently become a modish court figure, and it will no doubt do the like again after his restoration, and her banishment to the suburban brothels where she belongs.

In contrast, stepping forth to whip hypocrisy is never a very secure thing to do in Shakespeare: as Biron found in *Love's Labours Lost*, you can end up being exposed as a hypocrite yourself. This is the key: *Measure for Measure* and *Law-Tricks* both present more fallible rulers with the kind of human imperfections that Marston's plot systematically excludes from Altofronto. Day's Duke is shown to be not only just and well-meaning but also fatuously gullible: he dupes his son into bad behaviour, but the son then farcically dupes him back at the end of the play. In *Measure for Measure*, meanwhile, Vincentio is pointedly established in antithesis to Altofronto as a duke whose rule has not had any noticeably adverse effect on the bed-pressing fashion: the only person who remembers it as a lost golden age is, tellingly, the rake Lucio. The point is that in this play moral paragons are themselves inherently suspicious: the main action, undermining Angelo, calls into question the kind of blameless reputation that, in Marston's structure, would underwrite political authority.

Accordingly, Vincentio's politico-judicial philosophy is necessarily subtler than Altofronto's: 'He who the sword of heaven will bear | Should be as holy as severe' (3. 1. 517–18); the corollary is that those who cannot be absolutely holy must also not be absolutely severe. From the start he has accepted this view of the interrelated limitations on a ruler's private morality and his public action. It informs one of his stated reasons for leaving it to a deputy to curb the sexual incontinence over which he has, perhaps negligently, presided: 'Sith 'twas my fault to give the people scope | 'Twould be my tyranny to strike and gall them | For what I bid them do.' (1. 3. 35–7) In effect, he is perforce implicated in the evils that he himself procures— a point which is fundamental in the case of Angelo, whom he also promoted partly with a view to finding out whether he really was as pure as he seemed.

In this respect the Duke's choice of alter-ego is pertinent, because it establishes an iconic similarity with Angelo. As a friar, he has a holy outward appearance with an ordinary man inside; more specifically, the disguise also draws on the anti-Catholic rumours which circulated in the period, and which are latently invoked at several points in the play, about the promiscuity and sado-masochistic practices rife in monasteries and nunneries. (One of the spicier pictorial shop-signs of Elizabethan London showed a friar spanking a nun, obviously not entirely for disciplinary purposes.) The point is not that the Duke actually is the same kind of secret lecher as his deputy (at least, critics generally trust his word more than they do Lucio's on this issue), but that there are various processes, both narrative and metaphorical, operating to place the play's two central male figures in a continuum defined by their shared human fallibility rather than contrasting them as good and bad rulers, or men. This fact must and does limit the scope of Vincentio's executive action: by his own principle he can only be as severe as he is himself holy.

All these plays ultimately allow the possibility of forgiveness. It need not be done with good grace—Altofronto is as acid as Prospero will be to Antonio when he tells one corrupt courtier, 'You to my worst friend I would hardly give: | Thou art a perfect old knave' (5. 2. 197–8)—but the point is that it is done. Paradoxically it is not punishment but pardon that makes a man more like his maker: Angelo walks out of the examination of Froth and Pompey, hoping his colleague Escalus will 'find good cause to whip them all' (2. 1. 132); Vincentio reprieves Barnadine. Ultimately the plays end with a benevolence and a hope for redemption best expressed in a later phase of tragicomedy, when Posthumus tells the villain of *Cymbeline* (*c.* 1610), 'Live, | And deal with others better.' (5. 6. 420–1)

The Blackfriars: Politics and Gentility

The Malcontent's immediate impact was not to inaugurate a distinctive new genre born of one of late Renaissance Italy's baroque literary experiments, so much as to accelerate the progressive darkening of comedy in this period by encouraging the use of even more overtly 'tragic' material. In this most literary of the commercial theatre's phases, playwrights were certainly aware of the generic blurring involved, and sometimes called attention to it in prologues and epilogues. An unlikely example is *The Merry Devil of Edmonton*, a popular farce probably first staged by Shakespeare's company not long after *The Malcontent*: the play begins where *Doctor Faustus* ends, with a devil arriving to carry off a magician after the expiry of their soul-selling contract, but this time the conjuror cheats the devil, wriggles out of his bargain, and goes on to perform further magical feats in the rest of the play; the prologue underlines the juxtaposition of one genre's material with the other's outcome by asking the audience to await 'The comic end of our sad tragic show'. Responses to Marston were not all quite as mongrel as this, but in general the initial English interest in tragicomedy tended to be more intuitive than formal and theoretical; no other commercial-theatre play called itself a tragicomedy until 1608.

The summer of that year saw an abrupt end to Marston's writing career when he went to prison, leaving a half-started tragedy behind him. (He was to live on until 1634 as a respectable country clergyman, doing his best to obliterate all evidence of his former occupation as a dramatist.) By then, events had taken place which made it impossible for the stage to continue in his preferred mode of political satire, and which led indirectly to a new wave of tragicomedy. That Lent, the Blackfriars boy company, of which Marston was part-owner, had its final confrontation with the authorities. While most of the other playhouses were closed for the period of public self-denial, they not only caused a diplomatic incident by staging a two-part play by Chapman about recent French history, whose unflattering portrayal of the French monarchy gave offence, but also performed a comprehensive and scandalous satire on their own king. James was not amused: he swore that 'they should never play more, but should first beg their bread'.[2] In August the boys surrendered their lease on their indoor theatre, and it reverted to its owner, Richard Burbage. His new tenants were the company in which he was the leading actor, the King's Men.

These events probably contributed to a distinct modal shift in drama during the last years of the decade. Plays like Beaumont and Fletcher's *Philaster* (1609) and Shakespeare's *The Winter's Tale* illustrate the revitalized interest in tragicomedy, together with a change of tone from satirical to romantic: as in *The Malcontent*, the action develops through tragic events and situations to ultimate harmony, but now it no longer takes place in realistic settings but in distant times and foreign places which are often portrayed in a vague or idealized manner. The remoteness and lack of precision was probably the point: when Ben Jonson and others laughed at Shakespeare for setting a scene of *The Winter's Tale* on the sea-coast of Bohemia, they were drawing a mistaken equation between the dramatic location and the actual, land-locked middle-European country. The point of such settings was not to place the play in terms of topographical reality but to remove any overt application to English current affairs: 'Bohemia' or 'Sicily' or 'Iberia' really means 'elsewhere'. This would have been important in the wake of the Blackfriars boys' transgression, not least because these plays' withdrawal from identifiable settings did not mean an abandonment of political seriousness.

The Winter's Tale and *Philaster* both centre on acts of royal injustice: the state trial of Hermione for adultery, then a treasonable offence in a queen, and the King of Calabria's usurpation of the neighbouring kingdom of Sicily. The plays emphasize how far such events depend not only on the capricious or criminal will of the monarch but also on subjects who allow them to happen or retrospectively accept them. In the Beaumont and Fletcher play, the King cannot act against Sicily's rightful ruler, Philaster, for fear of reprisals from the people; eventually their rebellion is the agency through which Philaster is restored to the throne. The King is also shown to fret when his courtiers demand that he confine his orders to 'things possible and honest' (4. 4. 35). This became a key issue in *The Winter's Tale*, in which King Leontes twice commands courtiers to commit murder. The action draws a contrast between Camillo, who will not poison Hermione's supposed lover, and Antigonus, who follows his infanticidal orders to the letter and exposes her baby on the sea-coast: Antigonus gets eaten alive by the bear of the play's most famous stage direction, whereas Camillo has to go into voluntary exile but eventually returns home and marries Antigonus' widow. Antigonus is blameworthy because the monarch's power only extends as far as the subject's consent, so that the proper response to an immoral command is to refuse it as Camillo does. Though the standard accounts of these plays tend to emphasize their powerful emotional situations, they are also centrally concerned with early seventeenth-century England's key political issue, the limits of absolutism and the royal prerogative; after the events of 1608 it would have been difficult for the stage to debate this in a more realistic setting.

If the boys lost a theatre, the King's Men gained one, and this is also sometimes proposed as an explanation of the turn towards tragicomedy. The argument, which is usually advanced by critics who dislike the genre, has two main points. One is that the content of the plays was determined by the particular kind of audience which patronized the Blackfriars, and which tended, because of the higher admission prices, to be a less variegated and more socially exclusive clientele than the company served at the Globe. The other point is that the indoor playhouse may have offered more sophisticated stage technology than was available in their Bankside amphitheatre, making possible spectacular effects like the descent of Jupiter on an eagle's back in *Cymbeline* or the vanishing banquet in *The Tempest*. The result, it is suggested, was that dramatists began to write in terms of *coups de théâtre*, creating plays driven by a perceived need to find new ways to surprise and titillate their audience—a bit like the *Star Wars* kind of science fiction film where the quality of the special effects seems more important than that of the script. This accounts not only for the greater visual ambition which is taken to characterize these plays but also their predilection for 'strong scenes' like the statue of Hermione coming to life at the end of *The Winter's Tale*, or the notorious moment in *Philaster* when the title character, mad with passion, wounds his girlfriend.

This argument, that the Blackfriars theatre itself begat the genre, style, and tone of the plays performed there, needs to be treated with caution. It may contain an element of truth, not least because the fashion for romantic tragicomedy seems initially to have been associated with the King's Men alone, continuing with plays like

Beaumont and Fletcher's *A King and No King* (1611) and Fletcher and Shakespeare's *The Two Noble Kinsmen* (1613–14); it was noticeably later in the decade that comparable plays, such as *The Honest Man's Fortune* (Fletcher and Field, 1613), *A Fair Quarrel* (Middleton and Rowley, 1616), and *The Devil's Law–Case* (Webster, 1619), began to appear in other companies' repertories. But it is difficult to sustain the case that this was a symptom of a progressive gentrification of drama. Guarini had argued that one of the distinctive features of the genre was that it induced a response in the audience that was more temperate, and so more decorous, than that evoked by the two component genres: it combines and moderates their pleasures 'in order to prevent the listeners from falling into the excessive melancholy of tragedy or the excessive lewdness of comedy'.[3] In that respect it was indeed a more polite form well suited to an audience with a sense of its own gentility; yet in practice Guarini's particular mode of pastoral tragicomedy held little interest for London's indoor-theatre audiences.

Five years or so after Marston first experimented with his own inflection of the genre, Fletcher revisited Guarini with *The Faithful Shepherdess* (1608–9). As the title suggests, this is a tragicomedy more closely modelled on *The Faithful Shepherd*, and Fletcher summarized some of Guarini's genre theories in the preface to the published edition:

A tragicomedy is not so called in respect of mirth and killing, but in respect it wants deaths, which is enough to make it no tragedy, yet brings some near it, which is enough to make it no comedy; which must be a representation of familiar people, with such kind of trouble as no life be questioned, so that a god is as lawful in this as in a tragedy, and mean people as in a comedy.

It is an overtly literary play whose appeal lies more in its descriptive lyrical passages than in its narrative, which crawls slowly through a sludge of rhyming couplets: it probably reads better than it would act. Fletcher wrote it for the former Blackfriars boys in the period after their disgrace, when they were not begging their bread as the King had vowed but performing under new management and a new name at a different indoor playhouse; and the audience, drawn from the same privileged social constituency as frequented the Blackfriars, found it not to their taste. Fletcher's account of their response in the preface indicates that they wanted easier pastoral pleasures—'Whitsun ales, cream, wassail, and morris dances'—and perhaps that they were still unfamiliar with the genre, expecting a pastoral tragicomedy to be a burlesque of shepherds 'sometimes laughing together and sometimes killing one another', and were disappointed when the play failed to deliver this. Fletcher continued to be interested in recent Continental literature, and his reading of Guarini continued to inform his work; but when he moved on to write for the King's Men, it was accommodated to the more accessible romantic mode that he and Beaumont adopted with *Philaster*.

That kind of romance is something that playgoers would not have found at the Blackfriars before 1608, but it was an element in the repertory of the early Jacobean Globe. *Mucedorus*, an old relic of early 1590s theatrical taste, was revived by the King's Men in about 1605, and Shakespeare co-wrote *Pericles, Prince of Tyre* in the same style in 1607. Shakespeare criticism conventionally associates both of these plays with the Blackfriars tragicomedies that followed. *Mucedorus* includes an exciting scene in which a character exits pursued by a bear, and *Pericles* also has much in common with *The Winter's Tale*: in both plays Shakespeare stretches the plot across two generations, shaping its development around a wife's death and resurrection, and in both there is a correlation between sea voyages and changes of fortune; *Cymbeline*, moreover, shares *Pericles*'s resolution through theophany. The two later tragicomedies were obviously not just products of a new, rarefied Blackfriars taste; but it is just as unwise to conclude that after 1608 the Blackfriars was simply colonized by existing Globe tastes.

The critical tendency to treat *Pericles* as the first of a group of 'late romances' has made us much more aware of its similarities with the others than its differences. Writers of the 1630s considered it an artless play fit only for plebeian audiences, but it would be fairer to say that it adopts a deliberately naïve style and a rambling, episodic simplicity of construction as vehicles for its deeper emotional complexity. In contrast, it would be difficult to call the later plays anything more than *faux*-naïve, as if Shakespeare is playing at writing in a genre that he has already mastered in earnest. Their subject matter may resemble the old-fashioned 'winter's tales' of magicians, wicked stepmothers, and royal foundlings, but there is an overt artistry to them which Shakespeare had chosen not to use in *Pericles*: the rhythmical up-and-down of its successive episodes bears no resemblance to the complex architectonics of *Cymbeline* or *The Tempest*'s limitation to one day on one small island in accordance with the neo-classical unities. Obviously they draw on the company's earlier romantic repertory; but they also transform it.

What most distinguishes the tragicomedies of the Blackfriars period, both by Shakespeare and Beaumont and Fletcher, is a genteel quality not found in *Pericles*: they contain nothing like the raw, demotic stamp of the earlier play's brothel characters. This is not to say that the roles are more exclusively courtly—there are shepherds in *The Winter's Tale*, of course, and a 'country fellow' plays a crucial part in resolving the crisis of *Philaster*—but rather that courtly or gentry codes of conduct are central to the way the action is conceived. There is a preoccupation with honour as the control valve which regulates the relationship between the contradictory impulses of reason, will, and passion: the plays deal with what happens when the process malfunctions, as when Leontes or Philaster becomes madly jealous, but the ideal remains intact, an unquestioned standard against which the characters are judged and to which they will eventually return. A contrast with early Jacobean tragedy is instructive. There society and its codes actually break down, literally or metaphorically: in *King Lear* Britain disintegrates, at first in Lear's decision to divide the kingdom and finally through war, into a chaos where characters will embrace any expediency in the name of survival; in other plays, like Jonson's *Sejanus' Fall* or Webster's *The White Devil*, more stable societies are shown to depend on the same kind of unprincipled action by powerful men, and the plays are tragic partly because the state does not collapse (and so open the possibility of its replacement with something better). Thus the period's tragedies relativize all 'civilized' codes of action, whereas its tragicomedies objectify them: one genre deals with what men and women do, the other with what they should do, even if occasionally they fail. It could be argued, then, that the tragicomedies' new gentility is another sign of the new influence of a gentry audience: that the plays just reflected back at them, unchallenged, their own assumptions about behaviour and social order. If that is partially true, though, it cannot be the whole truth.

The most important fact about the King's Men after 1608 is that, unique among the London companies, they performed at two theatres, the Blackfriars in the winter for the beau monde and the

Globe in the summer for the great variety of people. Most of their plays were interchangeable between the two theatres: *Philaster*, *The Winter's Tale*, and *Cymbeline* were all performed at the Globe as well as the Blackfriars, though possibly without some of their mechanically achieved spectacle. This means that changing fashions in the repertory cannot be satisfactorily accounted for in terms of one theatre and one audience constituency alone; but equally the explanation need not be the same for both. Did the Globe audience think of these plays simply as a development from *Pericles*, and overlook their new element of gentility? We just don't know. It is difficult to assess their response, not only because they were a more heterogeneous group than the Blackfriars patrons, but also because we have very little precise information about them—in fact, we only know the name of one person, the astrologer Simon Forman, among the thousands who must have visited the Globe between 1608 and 1613 (when it burned down). But if we want to speculate, there is a King's Men practice from this period which may help us.

In the early 1610s the company frequently drew on a body of drama performed at even more exclusive venues than the Blackfriars. Under King James, the court developed a taste for masques, elaborate mythological or allegorical entertainments scripted by established literary figures such as Ben Jonson and enacted by courtiers to mark special occasions, complete with music, dancing, and lavish scenic spectacle. A number of Jacobean plays, belonging to various companies, include miniature inset masques as part of their representation of the court: one is performed in Beaumont and Fletcher's *The Maid's Tragedy* to conclude the celebration of an aristocratic wedding, and it is partly through staging a masque-like event that Prospero asserts his ducal authority in *The Tempest*. What is striking is the number of King's Men plays that contain material, sometimes embedded in a formal entertainment and sometimes not, which is related to specific masques recently performed at court. For example, *The Two Noble Kinsmen* restages the morris dance from Beaumont's *Masque of the Inner Temple and Gray's Inn* (20 February 1613), and Webster's *The Duchess of Malfi* draws its dance of madmen from Thomas Campion's *The Lords' Masque* (14 February 1613); elements of *The Maid's Tragedy* and *The Winter's Tale* may also have been written in with a view to using costumes from recent court shows.

Any interpretation of this phenomenon is bound to be conjectural, but the key issue is whether the plays' first audiences would have been aware that they were seeing recycled material. If not, these are simply cases of theatrical thrift in the service of spectacular plays; and if they did know, the fact that it happened more than once suggests that it was not considered an especially objectionable practice. It may, indeed, have been a minor added attraction: the opportunity to see parts of an entertainment originally laid on for a select group of lords and ladies at court. Though currently indeterminable, the point is interesting because the practice involved, of bringing to a wider audience drama that was initially available only to a higher echelon of society, corresponds with the custom the company instituted when it began its dual-theatre operation. If we accept that the post-1608 tragicomedies, with their technological demands and gentry appeal, were written for the Blackfriars and subsequently transferred to the Globe, then a part of the attraction for the amphitheatre crowd could have been a kind of 'snob value'; that would also explain why the genre was slow to catch on with other companies which performed in only one theatre. Like the crazes which followed *Tamburlaine* and *The Comedy of Humours* in the previous two decades, the fashion for tragicomedy may well have drawn in part on the opportunity which the plays, and in this case also the context of their performance, offered less privileged audiences to associate themselves imaginatively with a position of higher rank than they could ever enjoy in their own mundane lives.

Beyond Tragedy

Most of the critical debate about tragicomedy has been informed by a dissatisfaction, or even moral outrage, with its happy endings: it is treated as a 'comfort genre' that is bad for you in the same way that 'comfort food' is. The central experience in which it trades is audience relief at the transcendence of tragedy's limitations. In Guarini's theory of the genre, a tragicomedy's structural crisis would come in the fourth act, the point in *The Faithful Shepherd* where the tragic events intrude. Similarly in English tragicomedies, act 4 sees the outbreak of violence in *Philaster*, the enforced flight of Florizel and Perdita from their homeland in *The Winter's Tale*, and the point when Prospero nearly loses control in *The Tempest* by forgetting Caliban's plot to murder him. But what is still more important is the process by which things are drawn back from the edge.

Tragic characters are bound by the consequences of their and others' previous actions, and the genre's power often lies in our empathic engagement with their circumscription. In Heywood's *A Woman Killed with Kindness*, for example, Frankford is driven on by his jealousy and sense of honour to discover that his wife is indeed an adulteress, and then tormentedly wishes he could put their lives into reverse:

> O God, O God, that it were possible
> To undo things done, to call back yesterday;
> That Time could turn up his swift sandy glass
> To untell the days and to redeem these hours,
> Or that the sun
> Could, rising from the west, draw his coach backward,
> Take from the account of time so many minutes
> Till he had all these seasons called again,
> Those minutes and those actions done in them,
> Even from her first offence, that I might take her
> As spotless as an angel in mine arms.
> But O, I talk of things impossible,
> And cast beyond the moon.

$$(13. 52–64)$$

In life it is always too late to call back yesterday, but since Renaissance tragedy does not usually promote or evoke a happy acceptance of things as they are, it was natural that audiences should partly have longed for an alternative world where disaster might be averted. Shakespeare's mature tragedies, particularly *Othello* and *King Lear*, are masterly in their manipulation of this desire, teasing us in their closing scenes with the fruitless hope that Desdemona and Cordelia might be saved. In tragicomedy, in contrast, the wish is granted: the bonds of former deeds can be untied, even though the play cannot literally reverse time to undo them altogether. This is a genre in which the dead come back to life, but only because they have been drugged, like Imogen in *Cymbeline*, or are shamming, like Hermione in *The Winter's Tale*.

Consequently the genre depends even more overtly than tragedy or comedy on the dramatist's skill in plot management to achieve such an ending: it is not enough to offer some happy reversal of fortune which arbitrarily saves the characters. The plays' narratives often centre on things which the playwright keeps secret, sometimes from the audience and always from the main characters, so that a revelation at the end will transform the action from a tragic to a comic mode by retrospectively altering the nature of what has happened. In the fourth act of *A King and No King*, for example, King Arbaces teeters on the brink of incest with his sister Panthea, but new information emerges in the fifth which transforms both the foregoing events and the meaning of the title: instead of being a king who is unkingly in his sexual desires, Arbaces is literally no king but the unknowing product of a dynastic ruse, inserted as a baby into the royal line to ensure that the previous, impotent king had a male heir; this means that his relationship with Panthea is not incestuous after all, because she is not really his sister, and so he can become a king again by marrying her.

This is not, of course, to say that the genre works by deceiving us about the fundamental nature of the dramatic experience itself. With the notable exception of *The Mousetrap* (Agatha Christie's, not Hamlet's), a play will not live long in the repertory if it depends entirely for its effect on keeping secrets from the audience: it is a rare playgoer who does not know that it is futile to wait for Godot. On the contrary, some tragicomic plays announce their overall trajectory in titles like *A Bad Beginning Makes a Good Ending* or *All's Well That Ends Well*. This means that their pleasure is two-fold: at one level we are engaged with the characters, live with them through their sufferings, and rejoice with them when tragedy does not come to pass; but at another we are enjoying the literary spectacle of a playwright deftly overcoming all obstacles. Sometimes, then, the closing turn of the narrative surprises the audience, putting us on the same level as the characters, but sometimes we are allowed to anticipate it and take a more detached, self-consciously sophisticated view of its process. In *Philaster*, unlike in *Twelfth Night*, we are not told in advance that the page-boy is actually a lovesick girl, whereas in *Cymbeline* we know all along that the poison is only a sleeping potion, and that Imogen will eventually wake up: one is a conjuring trick, the other a juggling act, but they both elicit admiration for the dramatist's virtuosity.

For many modern critics, however, the genre's pleasures are debased ones. It is sometimes accused of a complacently acquiescent royalism in the way its conclusions encourage audiences to welcome the intervention of a benevolent figure of authority, whether it be the skilful dramatist outside the play or a manipulative disguised duke within it. Others seek to recover oppositional meanings from the plays' tragic content, a procedure which may be perverse in denying the whole point of the genre, but which is also characteristic of the debate in general: we tend latently to wish these plays were tragedies, so we favour the parts which pose problems and want to ignore or blame those which provide solutions. Such criticisms are unanswerable because within their own terms they are obviously right: tragicomedies do indeed cater to a desire not to have to face the hard realities of a tragic world, so the charge of irresponsible escapism must stand. Or at least, must stand so long as one accepts the assumption that the tragic experience is the most authentic, as modern critical sensibilities generally do. But this was not necessarily so for the early seventeenth-century audiences for whom the plays were written.

It is striking, but not very surprising, how far the iconography of Jacobean tragicomedy overlaps with that of Christianity. For example, the spectacle of the dead rising from their coffins or their graves, like Imogen in *Cymbeline* or Oriana in Fletcher's *The Knight of Malta* (1618), foreshadows the general resurrection that would take place, it was believed, at the end of the world; and the plots about deputies entrusted with power have their deep structure in the biblical parable of the talents (Matthew 25. 14–30), representing the Last Judgement, in which the servants have to invest their absent master's capital and give an account of themselves on his return. Some plays feature the benevolent intervention of the gods, albeit pagan ones—divine revelation is the principal agent of truth in *The Winter's Tale* and *Cymbeline*, and in *The Faithful Shepherdess*, a character is actually saved from death by a kindly river-god—and this mirrors the orthodox Christian view that history was informed by divine providence, that, as the Soothsayer puts it at the end of *Cymbeline*, 'The fingers of the powers above do tune | The harmony' (5. 6. 467–8) of its process.

This is not to suggest that the plays were written as Christian allegories, as some critics used to argue about *Measure for Measure*: Duke Vincentio is (more or less) merciful and forgiving precisely because he is not a perfect analogue of God. Indeed, these devices are often used for a comic effect, as when the drugged 'corpse' wakes up on the way to his own funeral in Middleton's *The Puritan* (1606), which would obviously have appeared inappropriate or even blasphemous to anyone expecting a covert religious meaning—not that a stage play would be the obvious first place to look in a culture that was already saturated with Christian texts and thought, ideas and images. That such material should have reappeared in drama indicates the depth of its penetration rather than any allegorical purpose; but equally its presence would have met with a degree of unconscious recognition. In tragicomedy, as in the Christian concept of history, virtue is always rewarded in the end, whatever its trials and afflictions on the way: in that sense, the experience the genre dramatized was just as authentic as that of tragedy, albeit within a different set of assumptions, and for a culture in which it was still possible for everyone to hope to be saved.

The Prodigal Father

In 1592, Robert Greene ended a dissolute life, his mind and pen swinging deliriously between self-pitying repentance and his usual jealous resentment of writers who had met with better fortune than he. In one of his deathbed writings, he warned his fellow playwrights, Marlowe, Nashe, and Peele, to beware of actors, 'those puppets... that speak from our mouths, those antics garnished in our colours'. Making a vain effort to foment the London theatre's first demarcation dispute, he pointed out that they were getting above themselves, writing their own plays and so taking work away from the professional dramatists; some of them may even have been committing plagiarism. His spleen was directed most of all at one relative newcomer: 'there is an upstart crow, beautified with our feathers, that with his "tiger's heart wrapped in a player's hide" supposes he is as well able to bombast out a blank verse as the best of you; and being an absolute *Johannes fac totum* [Jack of all trades], is in his own conceit the only Shake-scene in a country.'[1] It was an offensive outburst against Shakespeare—Henry Chettle, who saw the book through the press after Greene's death, was forced to apologize a few months afterwards—and it was typical of Greene's attitude to younger talents: four years earlier, he had been similarly rude about Marlowe, attacking the immorality of the *Tamburlaine* plays whilst also producing his own catchpenny imitation, *Alphonsus, King of Aragon* (1587–8). Yet if we lay aside our distaste for Greene's tone and our customary reverence for his target, it is possible that he may have had a sustainable perception, not about whether actors have the right to be dramatists, but about the kind of talent Shakespeare possessed.

The principal vehicle of Greene's attack is one of Shakespeare's characters: Queen Margaret from the *Henry VI* plays. In *Part 2*, she contributes to the virtuous Lord Protector's downfall, and so to England's slide into civil war, with an accusation of treacherous deceit: 'Seems he a dove? His feathers are but borrowed, | For he's disposèd as the hateful raven.' (3. 1. 75–6) And in *Part 3*, when she taunts the captured Duke of York with a handkerchief soaked in the blood of his murdered son, he replies with a powerful aria of pain and recrimination, which includes the play's best remembered line, then and now: 'O tiger's heart wrapped in a woman's hide' (1. 4. 138). Greene's taunting misquotation, and his central conceit of the feather thief, both derive from crucial moments when the Queen takes a hand in the demise of powerful men. His point takes its force from Shakespeare's emphasis on her violation of established hierarchies and gender roles, which make her a literal embodiment of the anarchy that is engulfing the kingdom. Her treatment of York shows harsh qualities supposedly alien to her sex—'Women are soft, mild, pitiful, and flexible— | Thou stern, obdurate, flinty, rough, remorseless,' (1. 4. 142–3)—and she adopts a masculine function in leading troops on the battlefield in place of her husband the King. Similarly, in Greene's analysis, Shakespeare the actor-puppet is unjustly supplanting his university-trained betters in presuming to write his own plays.

Many a terrible queen stalks the tragedies and history plays of the period: the group also includes Elinor in Peele's *Edward I* (*c*.1591) and Tamora in *Titus Andronicus*, and the character type remained fitfully potent as late as William Rowley's *The Birth of Merlin* (1622). These are all characters most notable, like Queen Margaret, for their defiance or supplanting of male authority and their rejection of the norms of feminine behaviour. Often they involve themselves in the man's world of politics, with disastrous results. In the anonymous history play cum political farce, *Look About You* (1599?), for example, Queen Eleanor of Aquitaine is said to have committed mass murder in starting a war: she is

> The tigress that hath drunk the purple blood
> Of three times twenty thousand valiant men,
> Washing her red chaps in the weeping tears
> Of widows, virgins, nurses, sucking babes.

(236–9)

It is striking, however, that the accusation is framed so that her victims include not only dead soldiers but also dead babies. These queens are portrayed as creatures of horror most of all in their deviation from the nurturing, maternal concept of womanhood: Queen Margaret is also associated with child murder (for all that some recent feminist critics have tried to reclaim her as a good mother), Tamora connives at Lavinia's rape, and the theme probably reached its ultimate pitch of *grand guignol* in *Edward I* when Queen Elinor uses poisonous snakes to suckle a nursing mother's breasts—not just a deed of physical horror but also a symbolic action which strikes against motherhood in attacking the part of the female body which most defines it.

It is not known for certain which of these characters came first (most early 1590s plays are notoriously difficult to date precisely), but the balance of probabilities favours Queen Margaret. If so, she was Shakespeare's most distinctive and original creation at the time Greene used her in his attack, a fine focus for his envy if not a very good illustration of his argument. Yet it is an originality which operates in terms already defined by an even more original recent work: as an empowered woman, Margaret is another exemplar of the fashion for hierarchical disruption which Marlowe had initiated with *Tamburlaine the Great*. In that sense, she was original but not revolutionary, and the response from other dramatists was simply to transplant her salient characteristics into other situations and other terrible queens; she did not have anything like the kind of shatteringly liberating effect of Marlowe's play. In this, as we shall eventually see, she may reflect the deeper point about Shakespeare which underlies Greene's nasty little diatribe.

Greene's concern was with how the rise of Shakespeare impinged on established playwrights like himself. That no longer matters: even an author's *amour propre* does not long outlive him. What is more interesting is the way Shakespeare later impinged, as an established playwright himself, on his successors. His personal career brought him a recognition and prosperity which few other dramatists enjoyed; and this was in part because, as Greene recognized, he was an insider in the group which controlled and profited from the theatre business, the senior actors and playhouse owners. By the end of the 1590s he was a moderately wealthy man whose name appeared as a selling-point on the title-pages of printed editions of his plays, and all this would have given him authority, not only as a respected commercial artist, but also as an institutional figure in his acting company. We shall never know how, or even whether, he exercised that authority. It is fascinating to speculate that he might have been involved in some kind of disciplinary action taken against Jonson during the War of the Theatres, as suggested in a piece of vague and unverifiable theatrical gossip passed on to posterity in the anonymous university play, *The Return from Parnassus, Part 2* (1602), or that he might have been the prime mover in the replacement of the mangled, pirated version of *Hamlet* printed in 1603 with the authorized edition of 1604; but ultimately we have no reliable documentary evidence about his dealings with the company or with other playwrights. What we can observe, though, is the shadow of his authority in the way his work affected their output.

Just as Shakespeare himself attracted gossip and anecdote when he became a known literary figure, so his plays became a focus for jokes and parodies, and none more so than *Hamlet*. It was perhaps inevitable that the authors of *Eastward Ho*, having given the name Gertrude to the goldsmith's daughter who makes a bad marriage, should have decided to call her footman Hamlet; and he is duly asked if he is mad when he gets angry. A year later, in *The Woman Hater* (1606), Francis Beaumont raised an intertextual laugh when two characters discuss the disappearance of a culinary delicacy:

> LAZARELLO Speak: I am bound to hear.
> COUNT So art thou to revenge when thou shalt hear:
> The fish head is gone and we know not whither.
>
> (2. 1. 344–7)

It is notable, however, that this is not the kind of lethal parody that was aimed at Marlowe in 1597. Both jokes work through incongruity: the mock-heroic juxtaposition of Shakespearian revenge rhetoric (from *Hamlet*, 1. 5. 6–7) with the picaresque story of a stolen meal, and the wryly inapposite naming of a tiny role after the longest and most challenging part in Shakespeare. Consequently they depend on a respect for the original play, rather than making it ridiculous as the Marlowe burlesques had done. There was never any time, from the ascendancy of Shakespeare until the closure of the London theatres in 1642, when younger dramatists successfully mocked his plays into outmoded oblivion; and this meant that those plays cast a long and not entirely comfortable shadow.

In the years leading up to Shakespeare's retirement, probably at the end of 1613, his work seems to have become the basis for what looks like a 'King's Men style': scenes and events which he created were redeployed, sometimes very ingeniously, by younger dramatists writing for the company. For example, Beaumont and Fletcher's *The Maid's Tragedy* includes a scene (5. 3) where the heroine, cross-dressed as a young soldier, visits the home of her ex-fiancé and has to argue with a servant in an effort to gain admittance; it is loosely based on the similar scene (4.5) between Coriolanus and Aufidius' servants in Shakespeare's play. Fletcher's *Valentinian* features a confrontation between a sexually undisciplined head of state and a heroine who compares her raped body with a desecrated temple, and who is told that she has no redress—'Justice shall never hear ye: I am justice' (3. 1. 34)—with the same chilling simplicity of Angelo's 'Who will believe thee, Isabel?' (2.4.154) in *Measure for Measure*. And the strangled heroine of Webster's *The Duchess of Malfi* revives, like Desdemona in *Othello*, for just long enough to say a few last pathetic words.

This is all very different from what Webster had done in *The White Devil*, written a few years earlier for a different company, when he created Cornelia's mad scene in terms overtly reminiscent of Ophelia's in *Hamlet*, significant herbs and all: 'There's rosemary for you, and rue for you, | Heart's-ease for you; I pray make much of it.' (5. 4. 71–2) Cornelia, a mother mourning her dead son, is Ophelia's antithesis, and the audience is evidently expected to recognize the similarity with Shakespeare's play; the effect is to enhance the situation's pathos, which will be psychologically important for one of the characters present. The examples from King's Men plays, in contrast, have no such allusive superstructure: there is none of *The White Devil*'s knowing precision, and the events are presented in their own right as if they are original; they just happen to have Shakespearian precedents. So the concern seems to be to reproduce known and reliable material, without making it too obvious that it has already been used elsewhere.

This is not an easily explicable phenomenon. None of the three examples comes from a bad play or an inexperienced author; none of them can be passed off as commercial competition, since all six plays involved belonged to the same company; and the number of instances (there are more that I have not cited) tends to complicate any argument for unconscious plagiarism. It is not altogether impossible that the dramatists hoped to make their scripts more acceptable by tailoring them to fit a presumed 'house style' in the company's existing repertory, or even that Shakespeare, at this late stage in his career, liked to see plays written 'his way'. But it seems far more likely that the influence operated, at least in part, at a less conscious level, not so much in the individual playwrights as in the play-writing culture to which they belonged: that ways of imagining events and scenes were increasingly determined by the practice of the most senior author still working in the theatre. This seems to be borne out by the way Shakespeare's imaginative hold tightened as he personally receded into history.

A good example of the extent of that influence is Middleton and Rowley's *The Changeling*, one of the most powerful tragedies written during the decade after Shakespeare's death. Middleton, who wrote the main plot, found in his source, a crime novella by John Reynolds, a bald story of a beautiful murderess named Beatrice-Joanna who employs an admirer, Deflores, to rid herself of an unwanted suitor, and ends up committing adultery with him. The character's name was soon worn down to Beatrice, at least in the authors' stage directions and speech prefixes, and one reason for this was probably that, in developing the story, Middleton began to think of her in terms of Shakespeare's Beatrice in *Much Ado About Nothing*. Both Beatrices are initially characterized in terms of an exaggerated antipathy for a man, Benedick and Deflores respectively, who is eventually to become her sexual partner; each has unwillingly to suffer his company as a result of an errand, in *Much Ado* when Beatrice is sent to fetch Benedick in to dinner and in *The Changeling* when Deflores is sent to tell Beatrice-Joanna that her fiancé has arrived; each Beatrice wants murder done and wishes she were a man, and each is reluctant to give the task to her preferred lover, respectively Benedick and Alsemero. Both plots also feature crucial moments which turn on the substitution of maidservant for mistress, though in somewhat different circumstances.

Middleton was further influenced by another Shakespeare play, which left its traces in the incongruous fact that the murder victim has told everyone that he has gone off in a gondola even though the play is set in Spain, and in another character's nautical description of making a pass at a woman: 'Yonder's another vessel, I'll board her; if she be lawful prize, down goes her topsail.' (I. I. 89–90) Middleton was obviously thinking of Iago on Othello's marriage: 'Faith, he tonight hath boarded a land-carrack. | If it prove lawful prize, he's made forever.' (I. 2. 50–1) As often with the better writers of the time, Shakespeare included, precise verbal echoes like this are the stigmata of a deeper imaginative influence, pinpricks that let through the light. The development of Deflores from the personable young man in the novella to the play's cunning, obsessive villain was evidently via *Othello's* 'honest' Iago: Middleton's character attracts the same ironically inappropriate epithet, and shares Iago's views, expressed to Roderigo, about the unlikelihood of female constancy. But Middleton's central transformation was to make him physically repellent: thus Beatrice-Joanna is made 'To fall in love with what she feared to look on' (I. 3. 98), as Brabantio says of Desdemona's affair with Othello. All these elements from Shakespeare are deeply embedded in the imaginative process which created the play's distinctive tragic situation; and it is possible to chart a similar enabling Shakespearian presence in the roots of other tragedies of the time, such as John Ford's *The Broken Heart* (1629) and *'Tis Pity She's a Whore* (1630).

Things were not always so subtle, however, or so rewardingly creative. The few readers of the tragedies of William Heminges, *The Jews' Tragedy* (1626) and *The Fatal Contract* (1639?), find much that is familiar: he was deeply indebted to his father John, who had helped to compile the first published collection of Shakespeare's plays, for his own work often seems to be little more than a patchwork of quotations from that volume. But it was not only lesser talents who made such obvious use of the plays. It is often, and sensibly, contended that in their own time people do not know that they are living through a period that will be known to history as 'late' in relation to what has gone before. Obviously the writers and playgoers of the 1620s and 1630s did not know the future, the outbreak of civil war and the closure of the theatres in 1642, any more than the characters of *Troilus and Cressida* know that Troy will burn and not be worn away by aeons of erosion as Cressida predicts. Yet in a sense they knew that their times were above all 'post-Shakespearian'. (A comparable example might be the way most aspects of late twentieth-century history were in some way a response to the 1960s.) The quarter-century of Shakespeare's career was a period of extraordinary creativity in English drama, and the perceived pre-eminence of his plays, reflecting the effortless superiority of a dead author, placed frustrated yet admiring younger dramatists in a double bind:

> Thy Muse's sugared dainties seem to us
> Like the famed apples of old Tantalus:
> For we, admiring, see and hear thy strains,
> But none I see or hear, those sweets attains.[2]

Shakespeare set a standard of excellence which their own work could not hope to reach, but by which it would nevertheless be judged. The result was a drama with a broad streak of nostalgia and a noticeable dependence on recycled materials.

In plays of the post-Shakespearian period you will find, among many others: a comic scene with a gravedigger, which contemporaries recognized as a lift from *Hamlet* (in Thomas Randolph's *The Jealous Lovers*); a father who affects disapproval of his daughter's low-born suitor, but, like Simonides in *Pericles*, communicates his true feelings to the audience in asides (Ford's *Perkin Warbeck*); a husband who is tempted by a villainous schemer into believing his wife has been unfaithful (Ford's *Love's Sacrifice*), and another who becomes insanely jealous after his wife seems to have disposed of one of his love-gifts (Philip Massinger's *The Emperor of the East*); a plot centred on lovers from rival families (Thomas May's *The Heir*); a queen whose husband irrationally accuses her of adultery with a court favourite whom she has praised (Richard Brome's *The Queen and Concubine*); characters who pretend to be statues and are reanimated by supposedly magical means (Massinger's *The City Madam*); a murderer who cannot wash his hands clean of blood which only he can see (*The Jews' Tragedy*); a clown who asks for guerdon and remuneration (Alexander Brome's *The Cunning Lovers*); and a group of artisans who are to perform before royalty, with a leading actor who wants to play all the parts (Thomas Rawlins's *The Rebellion*). (In case anyone has not guessed all the unspecified Shakespearian originals, look at: *Othello*; *Romeo and Juliet*; Hermione and the statue scene in *The Winter's Tale*; *Macbeth*; Costard in *Love's Labours Lost*; and Bottom and company in *A Midsummer Night's Dream*.) These examples include plots, events, lines of dialogue, jokes and comic set-pieces, spectacular scenes, and modes of human behaviour: Shakespeare's imaginative influence was pervasive.

My point is not the old and discredited one that post-Shakespearian drama lacks artistic integrity: recent criticism has, on the contrary, emphasized its seriousness and its deep engagement with the political crisis of its period. However, it is obvious that its narrative and dramatic horizons were substantially determined by the plays of the recent past, including not only Shakespeare but also some of his younger contemporaries like Jonson and Webster. (Readers of *The Heir* will quickly recognize the defining presence of *Volpone*, for example, and *The White Devil* was a pervasive influence on the imagination of James Shirley.) But this does not necessarily make it a barren, 'decadent' drama, more concerned with manipulating existing dramatic devices than with the direct representation of human experience. While one cannot rule out crude plagiarism in every case, it might be truer to say that Shakespeare simply continued to dominate the way in which human experience was conceived and dramatized. This is the import of John Dryden's remarks about him and his contemporaries, made later in the seventeenth century:

We acknowledge them our fathers in wit; but they have ruined their estates themselves before they came to their children's hands. There is scarce an humour, a character, or any kind of plot, which they have not blown upon: all comes sullied or wasted to us.... This therefore will be a good argument to us either not to write at all, or to attempt some other way. There is no bays [laurels] to be expected in their walks.[3]

Because the Shakespearian style was never effectively transcended in the way that Marlowe's had been, many later dramatists felt they had nowhere to go but back over the same ground he had marked out. This is where we come back to the quality that Robert Greene may have seen in the young Shakespeare in the days when he could still be thought of as an upstart crow.

Much of this book has been concerned with the defining contexts of Shakespeare's plays: they have been shown to be indebted not only to many of the ambient literary and theatrical practices of his time, but also to specific acts of originality by other playwrights, like Chapman's devising the comedy of humours or Marston's development of tragicomedy. The typical effect of such works was to spark off a vogue for commercial imitations of their surface features, like the wave of conqueror plays after *Tamburlaine*, but also to make fundamental, long-term changes in the kind of drama that could be written. Shakespeare never made that kind of impact on his contemporaries and heirs. He was an enormously successful writer: it is easy to document the commercial popularity and critical acclaim which greeted many of his plays, particularly *Henry IV, Part 1*, *Hamlet*, *Othello*, and *The Winter's Tale*, and to show the frequency with which other dramatists drew on his work. But on the whole that work was admired and imitated narrowly, as single plays whose influence is unusually easy to quantify in terms of the specific narrative features which were adopted. Shakespeare did not open out new and influential modes of drama in the way that Marlowe and Chapman and Marston had done, enabling later writers to exercise their own creativity in different ways; he only provided them with a treasure-house of new source material. In that sense, his was essentially a secondary talent (by which I do not mean a second-rate one): he was a great completer, maximizing the potential of other men's innovations and thereby, perhaps, beautifying himself with their feathers. The plays so adorned, seen in themselves, were among the greatest glories of English drama. Seen as part of a historical process, they were also its curse.

1. 'THE CAUSES OF PLAYS'

1. Stephen Gosson, *Plays Confuted in Five Actions*, in Arthur F. Kinney (ed.), *Markets of Bawdrie: The Dramatic Criticism of Stephen Gosson*, Salzburg Studies in English Literature: Elizabethan Studies 4 (Salzburg: Institut für Englische Sprache und Literatur, 1974), 150, 151, 181, 160, 161, 153.
2. E. K. Chambers, *The Elizabethan Stage* (Oxford: Clarendon Press, 1923), iv. 269.
3. *14 Elizabeth I c. 5*.
4. W. G. Hiscock, *A Christ Church Miscellany* (Oxford: privately published, 1946), 174.
5. John Marston, *Jack Drum's Entertainment*, in *The Plays of John Marston*, ed. H. Harvey Wood (Edinburgh and London: Oliver and Boyd, 1934–9), iii. 234.
6. Gosson, *Plays Confuted*, 169.
7. Ibid. 161.
8. Thomas Platter, *Travels in England*, 1599, tr. Clare Williams (London: Cape, 1937), 170.
9. Chambers, *The Elizabethan Stage*, iv. 190, 187; G. Gregory Smith (ed.), *Elizabethan Critical Essays* (Oxford: Oxford UP, 1904), i. 177, ii. 209, 35.
10. Stephen Gosson, *The School of Abuse*, in Kinney (ed.), *Markets of Bawdrie*, 97.
11. Chambers, *The Elizabethan Stage*, iv. 241.
12. E. K. Chambers, *William Shakespeare: A Study of Facts and Problems* (Oxford: Clarendon Press, 1930), ii. 341.
13. Chambers, *The Elizabethan Stage*, iv. 198–9; Gosson, *Plays Confuted*, 197.

2. NEW TRAGEDIES FOR OLD

1. Gosson, *Plays Confuted* and *The School of Abuse*, 181, 96–7.
2. Quoted by Thomas Lodge, *Wits Miserie, and the Worlds Madnesse* (London: Cuthbert Burby, 1596), H4ᵛ.

3. Comedy's Metamorphosis

1. Joseph Hall, *Collected Poems*, ed. A. Davenport (Liverpool: Univ. of Liverpool Press, 1949), 14.
2. John Chamberlain, *The Letters*, ed. Norman Egbert McClure (Philadelphia: American Philosophical Society, 1939), i. 32.
3. *Ben Jonson*, ed. C. H. Herford, Percy Simpson, and Evelyn Simpson (Oxford: Clarendon Press, 1925–52), i. 143.

4. Interlude: How to Write a Play

1. William Webbe, *A Discourse of English Poetry* (1586), in Smith, *Elizabethan Critical Essays*, i. 293.
2. Sir Philip Sidney, *An Apology for Poetry*, in Smith, *Elizabethan Critical Essays*, i. 197, 199.
3. Ibid. i. 199.
4. John Lyly, *Euphues*, in *The Complete Works of John Lyly*, ed. R. Warwick Bond (Oxford: Clarendon Press, 1902), i. 196.
5. Gosson, *Plays Confuted*, 160; George Whetstone, Dedication to *Promos and Cassandra*, in Smith, *Elizabethan Critical Essays*, i. 60.
6. *The Tragedie of Hamlet*, 1208–9, in William Shakespeare, *Hamlet*, ed. Horace Howard Furness, New Variorum Shakespeare (London and Philadelphia: J. B. Lippincott, 1877), ii. 64.
7. Sidney, *Apology*, i. 200.
8. Gosson, *Plays Confuted*, 169; 'Eutheo' (possibly Anthony Munday), *A Second and third blast of retrait from plaies and Theaters* (London: Henry Denham, 1580), H2^v; John Webster, *The Works*, ed. F. L. Lucas (London: Chatto and Windus, 1927), iv. 43.

5. The Hermaphrodite of Genres

1. Giambattista Guarini, *Compendio della Poesia Tragicomica*, tr. Damiano Pietropaulo, in Michael J. Sidnall (ed.), *Sources of Dramatic Theory* (Cambridge: Cambridge UP, 1991–), i. 153.
2. Chambers, *The Elizabethan Stage*, ii. 54.
3. Guarini, *Compendio*, i. 153.

Afterword

1. Chambers, *The Elizabethan Stage*, iv. 241–2.

2. Thomas Bancroft, epigram addressed to Shakespeare in *Two Bookes of Epigrammes, and Epitaphs* (London: Matthew Walbancke, 1639), D2ʳ.

3. John Dryden, *Of Dramatick Poesie, An Essay* (London: Henry Herringman, 1668), 65.

Further Reading

Anyone setting out to read beyond the handful of familiar and easily accessible plays by Shakespeare's contemporaries will need a guide-book, and also a map. For the former one could scarcely do better than G. K. Hunter's rich volume on the subject in the Oxford History of English Literature, *English Drama, 1586–1642: The Age of Shakespeare* (Oxford: Clarendon Press, 1997); Alexander Leggatt's *English Drama: Shakespeare to the Restoration* (London and New York: Longman, 1988) also provides a readable and informative if inevitably less comprehensive survey.

The fundamental scholarly materials about the plays and their contexts are assembled in E. K. Chambers, *The Elizabethan Stage*, 4 vols. (Oxford: Clarendon Press, 1923) and Gerald Eades Bentley, *The Jacobean and Caroline Stage*, 7 vols. (Oxford: Clarendon Press, 1941–68), respectively covering the periods before and after 1616; the former is, however, beginning to show its age. For visual materials these works are helpfully supplemented by R. A. Foakes's *Illustrations of the English Stage, 1580–1642* (London: Scolar Press, 1985). Useful specialized research tools include: Alfred Harbage and S. Schoenbaum, *Annals of English Drama, 975–1700* (2nd edn, London: Methuen, 1964; the third edition of 1989 contains updated material but is also riddled with misinformation, and is best avoided by the unwary or inexperienced); Thomas L. Berger, William C. Bradford, and Sidney L. Sondergard, *An Index of Characters in Early Modern English Drama* (revised edn, Cambridge: Cambridge UP, 1998); Edward H. Sugden, *A Topographical Dictionary to the Works of Shakespeare and his Fellow Dramatists* (Manchester: Manchester UP, 1925); and W. W. Greg, *A Bibliography of the English Printed Drama to the Restoration*, 4 vols. (London: Bibliographical Society, 1939–59).

The most extensive account of the preconditions and context for English Renaissance drama is John D. Cox and David Scott Kastan (eds.), *A New History of Early English Drama* (New York: Columbia University Press, 1997). The early part of the period is authoritatively covered in F. P. Wilson, *The English Drama, 1485–1585* (Oxford: Clarendon Press, 1968) and Howard B. Norland, *Drama in Early Tudor Britain* (Lincoln, Nebr. and London: University of Nebraska Press, 1995). The best books on the professional circumstances of Shakespeare's own time are Andrew Gurr, *Playgoing in Shakespeare's London* (Cambridge: Cambridge UP, 1987) and *The Shakespearian Playing Companies* (Oxford: Clarendon Press, 1996), and Richard Dutton, *Mastering the Revels: The Regulation and Censorship of Elizabethan Drama* (London: Macmillan, 1991). Emrys Jones, *The Origins of Shakespeare* (Oxford: Clarendon Press, 1977) remains the richest and most stimulating examination of the imaginative and intellectual beginnings of Shakespeare's creativity.

A compendious account of the relationship between Shakespeare's plays and his period's conceptions of genre is Lawrence Danson's *Shakespeare's Dramatic Genres* (Oxford: Oxford UP, 2000). The major recent works on Elizabethan and Jacobean tragedy are: J. W. Lever, *The Tragedy of State* (London and New York: Methuen, 1971); T. McAlindon, *English Renaissance Tragedy* (Basingstoke and London: Macmillan, 1986); Jonathan Dollimore, *Radical Tragedy* (2nd edn, Hemel Hempstead: Harvester Wheatsheaf, 1989); John Kerrigan, *Revenge Tragedy: Aeschylus to Armageddon* (Oxford: Clarendon Press, 1996); A. D. Nuttall, *Why Does Tragedy Give Pleasure?* (Oxford: Clarendon Press, 1996); and Michael Neill, *Issues of Death: Mortality and Identity in English Renaissance Tragedy* (Oxford: Clarendon Press, 1997). Useful books on Christopher Marlowe's plays include: Malcolm Kelsall, *Christopher Marlowe* (Leiden: E. J. Brill, 1981); Clifford Leech, *Christopher Marlowe: Poet for the Stage* (New York: AMS, 1986); and Emily C. Bartels, *Spectacles of Strangeness: Imperialism, Alienation, and Marlowe* (Philadelphia: Univ. of Philadelphia Press, 1993). William Urry's *Christopher Marlowe and Canterbury* (London and Boston: Faber, 1988) is not a conventional biography but helpfully explodes some of the myths that Marlowe scholarship is heir to. Richard Levin provides a thorough account of the early reception of *Tamburlaine the Great* in 'The Contemporary Perception of Marlowe's Tamburlaine' in *Medieval and Renaissance Drama in England* 1 (1984), 51–70, and Marlowe's literary relations with Shakespeare are analysed by M. C. Bradbrook in 'Shakespeare's Debt to Marlowe', which appears in her *Aspects of Dramatic Form in the English and the Irish Renaissance* (Brighton: Harvester, 1983), 17–31; for a rather more combative view, see also Wilbur Sanders, *The Dramatist and the Received Idea* (Cambridge: Cambridge UP, 1968). Thomas Kyd is Marlowe's poor relation in terms of the quantity of scholarship on his work, but is the subject of a solid study by Arthur Freeman, *Thomas Kyd: Facts and Problems* (Oxford: Clarendon Press, 1967), while Emma Smith's 'Hieronimo's Afterlife', in her edition of *The Spanish Tragedy* (Harmondsworth: Penguin, 1998), is a useful but not comprehensive survey of that play's continuing impact. Scott McMillin and Sally-Beth MacLean offer an interesting view of the late 1580s revolution in tragedy in *The Queen's Men and their Plays* (Cambridge: Cambridge UP, 1998).

The satirical mode of English comedy is studied by Brian Gibbons in *Jacobean City Comedy* (2nd edn, London and New York: Methuen, 1980), while Lyly's romantic and courtly treatment of the genre is the subject of Michael Pincombe's *The Plays of John Lyly: Eros and Eliza* (Manchester and

New York: Manchester UP, 1996). The best account of Ben Jonson is Anne Barton's *Ben Jonson, Dramatist* (Cambridge: Cambridge UP, 1984); other illuminating books are Martin Butler (ed.), *Re-Presenting Ben Jonson* (Basingstoke: Macmillan, 1999) and Ian Donaldson, *Jonson's Magic Houses* (Oxford: Clarendon Press, 1997). David Riggs, *Ben Jonson: A Life* (Cambridge, Mass. and London: Harvard UP, 1989) offers a good biography and more besides, and Jonson's relations with Shakespeare are the subject of Russ McDonald's *Shakespeare and Jonson, Jonson and Shakespeare* (Lincoln, Nebr. and London: Univ. of Nebraska Press, 1988). As with tragedy, the other significant 'non-Shakespearian' dramatist is less well served: it is typical that the most recent significant book on Chapman, A. R. Braunmuller's *Natural Fictions* (Newark: Univ. of Delaware Press, 1992), deals only with his tragedies. His importance as a writer of comedy is rarely acknowledged, and Millar MacLure's *George Chapman* (Toronto: Univ. of Toronto Press, 1966) is the most recent overview of his work as a whole.

The standard analysis of the aesthetics of English Renaissance drama is Madeleine Doran's *Endeavors of Art: A Study of Form in Elizabethan Drama* (Madison, Milwaukee, and London: Univ. of Wisconsin Press, 1954), a book deeply engaged in the intellectual culture of the time. A more brilliantly instinctive approach to Shakespearian dramatic structure lies behind Emrys Jones's *Scenic Form in Shakespeare* (Oxford: Clarendon Press, 1971), and more specialized studies of aspects of the subject include: Richard Levin, *The Multiple Plot in English Renaissance Drama* (Chicago and London: Univ. of Chicago Press, 1971); Anne Barton, *The Names of Comedy* (Toronto and Buffalo: Univ. of Toronto Press, 1990); and Janette Dillon, *Language and Stage in Medieval and Renaissance England* (Cambridge: Cambridge UP, 1998).

The seminal essay on the emergence of tragicomedy is G. K. Hunter's 'Italian Tragicomedy on the English Stage' in his *Dramatic Identities and Cultural Traditions* (Liverpool: Liverpool UP, 1978), 133–56. Two collections of essays challenge traditional perceptions of the genre: Nancy Klein Maguire (ed.), *Renaissance Tragicomedy* (New York, 1987); and Gordon McMullan and Jonathan Hope (eds.), *The Politics of Tragicomedy: Shakespeare and After* (London: Routledge, 1992). The most impressive study of Marston is Philip J. Finkelpearl's *John Marston of the Middle Temple* (Cambridge, Mass.: Harvard UP, 1969), and worthwhile books on the 'Beaumont and Fletcher' plays include: Eugene M. Waith, *The Pattern of Tragicomedy in Beaumont and Fletcher* (New Haven: Yale UP, 1952) and Gordon McMullan, *The Politics of Unease in the Plays of John Fletcher* (Amherst: Univ. of Massachusetts Press, 1994).

There is a detailed account of the Jacobean and Caroline reception of Shakespeare in Martin Wiggins, 'The King's Men and After', in Jonathan

Bate and Russell Jackson (eds.), *Shakespeare: An Illustrated Stage History* (Oxford: Oxford UP, 1996). Shakespeare's literary relations with his contemporaries are studied by E. A. J. Honigmann in *Shakespeare's Impact on his Contemporaries* (London and Basingstoke: Macmillan, 1982), and there is also a useful survey in Richard Proudfoot's 'Shakespeare and the New Dramatists of the King's Men, 1606–1613', *Stratford-upon-Avon Studies* 8: *Late Shakespeare* (London: Edward Arnold, 1966), 235–61. Martin Butler's *Theatre and Crisis, 1632–1642* (Cambridge: Cambridge UP, 1984) is the seminal work on the later period, and R. L. Smallwood provides a valuable case study of Shakespearian influence in *'Tis Pity She's a Whore* and *Romeo and Juliet'*, *Cahiers Élisabéthains* 20 (1981), 49–70.

Note: This is not intended to be a full bibliography of all the plays discussed in this book, only a modest list of the editions which have been used for reference.

R. B., *Apius and Virginia*, ed. Ronald B. McKerrow (Oxford: Malone Society, 1911).

Beaumont, Francis, *The Woman Hater*, ed. George Walton Williams, in Fredson Bowers (gen. ed.), *The Dramatic Works in the Beaumont and Fletcher Canon*, vol. 1 (Cambridge: Cambridge UP, 1966).

Beaumont, Francis, and John Fletcher, *Philaster*, ed. Andrew Gurr, Revels Plays (London: Methuen, 1969).

Chapman, George, *The Comedies*, gen. ed. Allan Holaday (Urbana, Chicago, and London: Univ. of Illinois Press, 1970); *The Revenge of Bussy D'Ambois*, in Katharine Eisaman Maus (ed.), *Four Revenge Tragedies*, Oxford English Drama (Oxford: Oxford UP, 1995).

Clyomon and Clamydes, ed. W. W. Greg (Oxford: Malone Society, 1913).

Day, John, *Law-Tricks*, ed. John Crow (Oxford: Malone Society, 1950 for 1949).

Edward the Fourth (London: John Oxenbridge, 1599).

Fair Em, the Miller's Daughter of Manchester, ed. Standish Henning (New York and London: Garland, 1980).

Fletcher, John, *The Faithful Shepherdess*, ed. Cyrus Hoy, in Fredson Bowers (gen. ed.), *The Dramatic Works in the Beaumont and Fletcher Canon*, vol. 3 (Cambridge, 1976); *Valentinian*, in Martin Wiggins (ed.), *Four Jacobean Sex Tragedies*, Oxford English Drama (Oxford: Oxford UP, 1998).

Greene, Robert, *Friar Bacon and Friar Bungay*, ed. J. A. Lavin, New Mermaids (London, 1969); *James IV*, ed. Norman Sanders, Revels Plays (London: Methuen, 1970); *Selimus*, ed. W. Bang (Oxford: Malone Society, 1909 for 1908).

Heywood, Thomas, *The Fair Maid of the West*, ed. Robert K. Turner, jun., Regents Renaissance Drama (London: Edward Arnold, 1968); *If You Know Not Me, You Know Nobody, Part 2*, ed. Madeleine Doran (Oxford: Malone Society, 1935 for 1934); *A Woman Killed with Kindness*, ed. R. W. van Fossen, Revels Plays (London: Methuen, 1961).

Jack Straw, ed. Kenneth Muir and F. P. Wilson (Oxford: Malone Society, 1957).

Jonson, Ben, *Ben Jonson*: Complete Critical Edition, ed. C. H. Herford, Percy Simpson, and Evelyn Simpson, 11 vols. (Oxford: Clarendon Press, 1925–52).

A Knack to Know an Honest Man, ed. H. de Vocht (Oxford: Malone Society, 1910).

Kyd, Thomas, *The Spanish Tragedy*, in Katharine Eisaman Maus (ed.), *Four Revenge Tragedies*, Oxford English Drama (Oxford: Oxford UP, 1995).

Locrine, ed. Ronald B. McKerrow (Oxford: Malone Society, 1908).

Look About You, ed. W. W. Greg (Oxford: Malone Society, 1913).

Lyly, John, *The Complete Works*, ed. R. Warwick Bond (Oxford: Clarendon Press, 1902).

Marlowe, Christopher, *Dido, Queen of Carthage*, ed. H. J. Oliver, Revels Plays (London, 1968); *'Doctor Faustus' and Other Plays*, ed. David Bevington and Eric Rasmussen, Oxford English Drama (Oxford: Oxford UP, 1995). All quotations from *Doctor Faustus* are from the A-text.

Marston, John, *'The Malcontent' and Other Plays*, ed. Keith Sturgess, Oxford English Drama (Oxford: Oxford UP, 1997).

The Merry Devil of Edmonton, in C. F. Tucker Brooke (ed.), *The Shakespeare Apocrypha* (Oxford: Clarendon Press, 1908).

Middleton, Thomas, *The Phoenix*, in *The Works*, ed. A. H. Bullen, vol. 1 (London: John C. Nimmo, 1885); *'Women Beware Women' and Other Plays*, ed. Richard Dutton, Oxford English Drama (Oxford: Oxford UP, 1999).

Munday, Anthony, *The Downfall of Robert, Earl of Huntingdon*, ed. John C. Meagher (Oxford: Malone Society, 1965 for 1964); *Fedele and Fortunio, the Two Italian Gentlemen*, ed. Percy Simpson (Oxford: Malone Society, 1910 for 1909).

Rowley, Samuel, *When You See Me, You Know Me*, ed. F. P. Wilson (Oxford: Malone Society, 1952).

Shakespeare, William, *The Complete Works: Compact Edition*, ed. Stanley Wells, Gary Taylor, John Jowett, and William Montgomery (Oxford: Clarendon Press, 1988). I have not always felt bound to follow this edition's choice of character names, such as Robin Goodfellow (for Puck) and Innogen (for Imogen). *King Lear* is quoted from the revised (Folio) version here printed as *The Tragedy of King Lear*.

Suckling, Sir John, *The Plays*, ed. L. A Beaurline (Oxford: Clarendon Press, 1971).

The Taming of a Shrew, ed. Stephen Roy Miller, New Cambridge Shakespeare (Cambridge: Cambridge UP, 1998).

The Troublesome Reign of King John, ed. J. W. Sider (London and New York: Garland, 1979).

A Warning for Fair Women, ed. Charles Dale Cannon (The Hague: Mouton, 1975).

Webster, John, *The Works*, ed. David Gunby, David Carnegie, and Antony Hammond, vol. 1 (Cambridge: Cambridge UP, 1995).

Wilson, Robert, *The Cobler's Prophecy*, ed. A. C. Wood (Oxford: Malone Society, 1914).

The entries in this index relating to English plays written between 1500 and 1642 include their approximate date of original composition and first production.